# Be All You Can Be

## Edward Vaughn

iUniverse LLC
Bloomington

# BE ALL YOU CAN BE

iUniverse books may be ordered through booksellers or by contacting:

iUniverse
1663 Liberty Drive
Bloomington, IN 47403
www.iuniverse.com
1-800-Authors (1-800-288-4677)

ISBN: 978-1-4759-9728-6 (sc)
ISBN: 978-1-4759-9729-3(e)

Printed in the United States of America

iUniverse rev. date: 6/25/2013

# Prologue

We are all occasionally exposed to potentially hazardous physical and/or mental health conditions; and there is one, although avoidable and treatable, to which far too many people have become afflicted. Despite our awareness of its potentially destructive consequences, it continues to be on the rise, creating unhappy and unhealthy lives for its sufferers, and sadness for those who care about them. This hazardous condition is *obesity*.

According to the Center for Disease Control and Prevention, obesity can also serve as the **gateway** to many other debilitating physical and mental health disorders, including serious cardiovascular and neurological problems, diabetes, joint problems, strokes, various types of cancer, osteoarthritis, dysfunctioning of some of the body's key organs, and a wide range of mental, psychosocial, and economic problems.

Some people acquire the genesis of this disorder early in life, many genetically and/or congenitally, and they often later suffer from its dangerous consequences of unhealthy, unhappy, and shortened lives. There are also many more who, at some later point in life, allow themselves to become obese due to an **addiction to food**, usually of the worst and most fattening kinds, and/or

**excessive alcohol consumption** in order to self-medicate their anxiety (irrational fear), depression (internalized anger), and stress (feelings of extreme pressure).

As their obesity grows, these unfortunate people usually further succumb to sedentary and unhealthy lifestyles. While the initial causes of obesity may vary, the eventual results are about the same for all its sufferers... **unhappy and unhealthy lives.**

Despite the obvious and destructive consequences of their obesity, many foolish people choose to deny that they even have a problem and give in to their compulsions of pursuing the path of least resistance. Their general attitude toward their personal health seems to be: *If it feels good, do it (e.g., overeating and/ or eating unhealthy food items, abusing alcohol, and/or leading a sedentary lifestyle);* or *If it doesn't feel good, don't do it (e.g., exercising and consuming healthier, although not necessarily the most taste-appealing, food items, intelligently controlling alcohol consumption), and maintaining physical fitness.*

"Snake oil" peddlers have been capitalizing on this ubiquitous disorder for years through solicitations on the Internet, television, and junk mail with highly exaggerated promises of quick and easy fixes in the form of pills (which some will foolishly wash down with beer or sugar loaded drinks) that usually accomplish little to nothing, machines and devices that most people don't even use after purchasing them (many winding up being used as junk or clothing collection spots), and some unusual and often weird diets that range being minimally to totally *in*effective and may cause other health and nutritional problems. **"Snake oil" does not work!**

Fortunately, there are strategies that can help to overcome this condition rather than allowing it to negatively affect and undermine so many aspects of the afflicted person's life. Many responsible individuals choose to not surrender to obesity, but fight it with all of their spiritual, mental, and physical strength. They are the ones who usually **win** this sometimes difficult and painful battle, and they are rewarded with much **healthier bodies and minds, and longer and happier lives!**

Regardless of the means obesity sufferers employ to reverse this destructive process and bring their bodies and minds into a healthier condition, their chances for success are greatly enhanced if they have a deeply inspired and passionate commitment to *be all they can be.*

The following story is about Faith Thomas, a young girl from Fayetteville, North Carolina who was obese at birth and most aspects of her early life were miserable as a result. This terrible obesity produced hurtful ostracizing, teasing, and social rejection from her peers; an anger-driven personality, extremely low self-esteem, and some potentially dangerous early physical consequences... **until she discovered she had the power to change!**

If you or someone for whom you care are experiencing the miseries of obesity, I hope this story will inspire you or the obese person for whom you care, to overcome and break free from this difficult physical and psychological imprisonment, enjoy a happier and healthier life, and **be all you can be!**

Now that I've told you things you probably already knew, I hope you enjoy the story and a happier new life!

**Ed Vaughn**

# Chapter One

"**O**h my God, Kenny, this pain is killing me and I just can't take any more of it, so please, please, honey, hurry up and get me to the hospital quick before I die!" Rebecca Thomas screamed as she was experiencing the agonizing labor pains of childbirth.

Her shrill screams were echoing throughout the small Green Acres Trailer Park, and the neighbor in the trailer next to theirs angrily shouted at them, "Hey you people, it's damned near midnight and we're trying to get some sleep. Some of us don't have welfare and have to work for a living, so y'all better knock off that noise right now or we're gonna call the cops!"

Rebecca's husband, Kenny, angrily yelled back, "You can call the damned cops if you want to, you son of a bitch, but my poor wife's having a baby and she's hurting real bad, so leave us the hell alone and mind your own damned business!"

Kenny gently held Rebecca in his arms, patting and trying to comfort her as she moaned in pain and held his hand in a death grip. "Just keep on pushing real hard, Honey, and it'll be over with soon. Our baby girl is about to come out of your belly *any second now; and when she does, I'll rush both of you to the hospital right away and I promise that you're gonna be okay."*

*The curious eyes of a sleepy six-year-old boy in a nearby trailer peeked between tattered curtains as the trailer park seemed to vibrate in the night with screams and loud voices. He pulled a blanket over his head, hoping the shouting wouldn't awaken and upset his poor and tired working mom.*

Finally, after nearly three hours of terribly painful labor, at a little past midnight on a freezing and snowy early December morning in the small and shabby trailer park located in Bonnie Doone, one of the more underprivileged residential neighborhoods of Fayetteville, North Carolina, Rebecca Thomas let out a final loud and shrilling scream.

The baby, whom her parents named Faith Anne Thomas, then exited from the comfort and safety of her mother's womb without any professional medical assistance, and entered into a trouble-filled life inside her parents' run-down, rented, single-wide trailer. Since they hadn't paid the phone bill for several months, their service had been terminated and they were not able to call 911 for help.

Faith's father, Kenny Thomas, a disabled former Navy medical corpsman, alcoholic, drug addict, and chronically unemployed construction worker, carefully wrapped his ailing wife and their newborn baby daughter in blankets, with the umbilical cord still connecting them, and gently placed them in the front seat of his beat-up, twenty-year-old rusted Datsun pickup truck.

When Kenny turned the ignition key to start his truck, his battery was deader than a doornail. He then frantically knocked on the doors of several of his neighbors' trailers, begging someone to give him a jump-start.

After he was finally able to persuade a neighbor to help him start his truck, Kenny, Rebecca, and baby Faith left the trailer park and raced towards the hospital. Then, nearly a mile from the Cape Fear Valley Regional Medical Center, the old pickup truck's engine sputtered a couple of times, died, and the truck rolled to a stop.

Exasperated, Kenny banged his fists on the steering wheel and tearfully cried aloud, "Damn it all…now we're out of gas! What the hell else in my screwed up life is gonna go wrong next?"

He tearfully said to Rebecca, "You stay here with the baby, honey, while I run to the hospital and get us some help. Y'all just hang in there and I'll get back to you as fast as I can. Don't worry…I love you both and I promise you're gonna be okay."

Kenny hugged his moaning, badly hurting and bleeding wife and crying baby daughter, jumped out of the truck, and quickly ran through the heavy snowfall, slipping, sliding, and falling on the icy road several times before finally reaching the hospital emergency room.

Exhausted, crying, and bleeding from his several painful falls, he hysterically pleaded to the emergency room head nurse, "Help me, m'am; please help me! My truck just ran out of gas, and my poor wife and newborn baby girl are down the road in it. They're cold and hurting, and need help; and they need it right now! Please, please get someone to take me to where they are and get them here before they freeze to death!"

The head nurse called for a hospital security staff member who immediately led Kenny to a waiting ambulance. Within the hour, Rebecca and her baby girl had been picked up by the ambulance and were safely inside the hospital.

Rebecca was cleaned up, treated, and tucked into a warm and comfortable bed in the hospital's maternity ward, and baby Faith was cleaned up and treated in the nursery. Both mother and daughter were safe and well.

As his wife and newborn baby girl were being taken care of, a badly hurting Kenny was downstairs in the emergency room receiving treatment for his badly cut knees and elbows, sprained back, and many scrapes and skinned spots on his head, legs, and arms that had resulted from his slipping and falling numerous times on the icy road.

After Kenny's injuries had been cleaned, stitched, and bandaged, the emergency room doctor prescribed Kenny's favorite and much-welcomed pain medication of Percocet, one of several drugs to which he had become badly addicted over the past few years.

When LaRita Parker, the nurse in charge of the nursery, cleaned, examined, and weighed baby Faith, she was amazed to find that the four-hour-old baby weighed nearly fifteen pounds! She remarked to her assistant, "Good golly, Margaret, this little gal is a real cutie, but in my over twenty years of pediatric nursing, she's absolutely the heaviest newborn baby I've ever seen!"

Margaret replied, "Yep, LaRita, this little fatty is going to have some real serious problems going through life if she doesn't thin out some." Little did the nurse know how prophetic her remarks were on this, the first day of Faith's earthly life!

From the beginning, baby Faith had an insatiable appetite. Although her mother's breast milk was productive and would have been sufficient for the average sized infant, it wasn't nearly enough to satisfy this baby, so she had to be given baby formula supplements from the start.

The family returned home from the hospital a few days later and Faith continued to scream constantly for more nourishment than her mother was able to provide.

Rebecca would give Faith increasingly frequent and larger supplements of baby formula to fill her tummy and quiet her so she and her husband could sleep. Life with the Thomas family had become almost intolerably hectic since Faith's birth!

\*\*\*

After the turmoil of Faith's birth was over and her parents had left the trailer park for the hospital, the night was again quiet as the six-year-old little boy lay on a small cot trying to fall back asleep. As usual, his thoughts strayed back to a better time and place in his earlier life. In his mind, he happily recalled and pictured his former warm and friendly home with its manicured lawn and many beautiful flowerbeds.

There was a large barbeque grill on the back patio where his dad, attired in his bib apron and tall funny hat, would play chef and often manage to catch the hamburgers on fire. He, his mom, and dad would all laugh as they ate the charred burgers and played games together.

Wallace Morgan Cochran regularly attended Sunday school and church with his parents, and they said their nightly prayers together before the beautifully framed picture of Jesus which hung on the wall of Wallace's bedroom.

His beautiful and loving mother had always tried to make each day a happy and interesting adventure for little Wallace. She would often take him to the movies and have an ice cream cone together afterwards; take long walks with him where she would teach him the names of the trees, flowers and birds they saw, and visit the library to pick out an armful of books to take home and read together. By the time he was four years old, his mother had taught him to read and write on a second grade level.

His dad had promised him a puppy for his next birthday; but before that happened, everything in his world suddenly changed, and Little Wallace and his mother would quickly find themselves facing a very different and difficult life.

Wallace's father, Bertram Cochran, had been a previously well liked and trusted businessman, but was later found out to be a petty white collar criminal...a con artist; however, even as a criminal, he was pretty much of a failure. He wasn't able to continue soliciting a large enough number of fresh investors. His efforts to hide the funds previously bilked from the few investors he had were pitifully unsuccessful, and they were closing in on him for money he wasn't able to deliver.

Bertram was finally arrested and charged with numerous counts of running a Ponzi scheme that he pulled on several local retirees. He was convicted on criminal charges under North Carolina State law and sentenced to four and a half years in the state prison, and was also facing possible Federal charges from the SEC in connection with the scheme that he had been running for the past five years.

He, his wife, Janice, and their son, Wallace, had lived a comfortable, but modest, lifestyle in their middle-class suburban Fayetteville home, even though Bertram had maintained large cash balances in several out of the area banks. Janice was oblivious to his criminal activities and to the substantial amount of illegal cash he had secretly stashed away.

Now, with Bertram serving time in prison and all of his and Janice's assets having been seized by the authorities, Janice was forced out of their comfortable home and fled with her young son to the only home they could afford, a small singlewide trailer in a rundown trailer park in the impoverished Bonnie Doone neighborhood of Fayetteville.

\*\*\*

Faith's almost constant hunger for food continued to increase and by the time she was three years old she weighed over fifty pounds, her face was so large and puffy that her eyes appeared to be nearly swollen shut, and she waddled like a fat little duck when she walked.

Out of frustration over Faith's rapidly growing obesity, chronic abdominal pain, and nearly insatiable appetite, Rebecca would frequently take her to the Cape Fear pediatric clinic as a Medicaid patient and desperately try and get help for her; however, no significant change occurred and Faith only continued to grow more obese.

The pediatrician's routine advice to Rebecca was for her to change her daughter's diet to a less fattening one and encourage her to exercise. But the hunger pains continued and the weight gain increased until Rebecca finally gave up and accepted that there was no hope for Faith's steadily increasing hunger and weight gain to change, so she would give her more and whatever kind of food she cried for just to shut her up.

When she began kindergarten at the age of five, Faith weighed over eighty pounds and was ridiculed and teased for her obesity by her little classmates, and even by her insensitive and not very bright teacher. While teaching the children the alphabet, the teacher thought it was cute to point out to the class that Faith's initials spelled FAT! As the children broke out in laughter, poor Faith broke out in tears.

Each morning when Rebecca would walk with Faith to catch the school bus, the chubby and waddling five-year-old would sob, cling to her mother, and plea to let her stay at home and not have to go to school; but Rebecca refused her pleas and made her get on the school bus.

Faith had already sadly learned what the day with her classmates would likely bring...more cruel teasing about her obesity, which would produce embarrassment, humiliation, and a steadily lowering of her sense of self-esteem, all of which was becoming devastating to the pathetic child's early social development.

As soon as she got on the bus, the children would begin their taunting of Faith by teasing her with cruel jokes directed at her obesity such as "Fatty, Fatty, is an elephant your daddy?" "Piggy, Piggy, why are you so biggy?" The school bus driver would even laughingly join in on the fun the children were having at Faith's emotional expense.

These and the other cruel teasing she received which always focused on her obesity never failed to bring Faith to tears. The poor child always had to sit by herself on the bus with her head down and tears streaming down her sad face, because none of the other children wanted to be seated next to her.

\*\*\*

Four years later, Bertram Cochran finally returned from prison to his home and family in Fayetteville as a changed man, but the change wasn't for the better. Wallace and his mother weren't reunited with the once kindly, church-going, polite businessman, loving husband and caring father they remembered him as being prior to his incarceration; instead, the prison experience had transformed him into a loud, cocky, hostile, blatantly amoral, and generally unpleasant jerk.

On the day he returned home, Bertram rolled up his

shirt sleeves and proudly showed off his prison tattoos to his wife and son. On his right forearm he had a tattoo of a naked woman with his wife's name, Jan, beneath it; and on his left forearm he had a lightning bolt with the name 'Wally' above it.

He also proudly announced to them that he had finally "seen the light" and become an Atheist while in prison, and didn't want his wife and son to attend church any longer. He said, "We're not gonna let those phony, holy-rolling, do-gooder, money-grabbing church hypocrites take another dime of our money."

He told his wife, who had always called him and her son by their formal given names that he was to now be called Bert and their son called Wally. He said that if he and his son were going to be the tough guys they need to be in order to survive in this tough life, they needed to be called by a tougher name.

"I'm sorry, son, but Wallace is a pansy-sounding name and we've gotta be tough to get along in this tough and rotten world we're living in." Bert would then always refer to and address him as 'Wally', and would nag and belittle Janice any time she addressed or referred to their son as Wallace or to him as Bertram.

Bert usually stayed in bed until past noon every day, and then would clean himself up and leave the trailer later in the afternoon. When he returned home late at night, he typically had money in his pockets and was usually in an alcohol-induced jovial mood. Little Wally would toss in his bed trying to block out the noisy sexual activity he couldn't help hearing coming from the other side of the thin trailer wall. Then the babies started coming.

# Chapter Two

From the very beginning of her school life, Faith didn't adjust well to learning and socializing, and was often directed to sit alone at a separate table in the classroom since she required extra help from the teacher's aide.

Her problem wasn't that she was unable to learn, but she was filled with so much anger, embarrassment, and anxiety over the snide and hurting remarks being directed at her by her classmates, and sometimes even by her insensitive teacher, about her obesity that she was not able to focus sufficient attention to her schoolwork.

Despite her poor adjustment and learning difficulties, Faith was automatically advanced on to the next grade with what amounted to barely passing work. By the time she had reached the third grade, she was performing at barely above a first grade level, had been labeled as learning disabled, and weighed nearly one hundred pounds.

Faith's chronically unemployed and, ironically, emaciated father was continuing in his struggle to cope with an increasing addiction to alcohol and pain medications, and had even made an unsuccessful attempt to bring his miserable life to an end by cutting his left wrist. But instead of killing himself, the poor loser wound up with a badly damaged nerve that caused him to lose the functioning of his left hand.

After eight years as Faith's father, Kenny had endured as much of the stress from living in the hectic home as his tattered nerves, chronic depression, poor health, alcoholism, and drug addiction could tolerate.

Finally, early one morning while Rebecca and then eight-year-old Faith were asleep, Kenny quietly slipped out of their trailer and deserted his wife and daughter. He was never heard from until nearly a year later, when Rebecca received a notice from the police that he had been found dead from a drug overdose while living under a bridge on the outskirts of Orlando, Florida.

Upon learning of her estranged husband's death, Rebecca's very angry and cold response was, "It serves the dirty bastard right for running out on us the way he did, and I hope he burns in hell for it."

Rebecca was an orphan who had no other family members to turn to for help, so she and Faith continued to live alone in the trailer, subsisting on food stamps; a government rent subsidy, Medicaid, charity handouts, and social security disability compensation for a feigned back injury.

In an attempt to numb the mental anguish of their miserable living situation, an increasingly unhappy Rebecca also turned to a gluttonous consumption of fattening foods and alcohol, and soon became severely obese, very angry, and depressed like her daughter.

Rebecca would average twelve to fifteen hours of sleep daily, spending virtually no constructive time with her daughter in their disheveled little trailer home. Instead, the times when they were both awake in their home were mostly spent in stuffing themselves with Twinkies and other sugar laden snacks, drinking fattening beverages like Mountain Dew and beer, and lying on the couch watching television between naps.

Her caring third grade teacher, Cheryl Peters, was sympathetic towards Faith and tried to provide her with some sorely needed personal attention. She intuitively questioned the diagnosis that had been previously made of Faith's learning disability and had her take an abbreviated Wechsler intelligence test for children.

The results of the test indicated that Faith was highly intelligent with an IQ in the 150+ range, although the below standard quality of her schoolwork didn't reflect it. She then scheduled a parent-teacher conference with Rebecca to discuss Faith's social, learning, and health issues.

When Rebecca, who by then weighed over two hundred pounds, waddled into the teacher's classroom with Faith, Ms. Peters quickly realized that Faith's problem went well beyond her school issues.

At Ms. Peters' first mention of Faith's obesity, Rebecca became very hostile and defensive; then suddenly jumped up, gave Ms. Peters the middle finger and shouted, "You're nothing but a mean, nosey, and skinny bitch and you just don't like my child. You should mind your own damned business and keep your prejudicial attitude which, in my opinion, isn't worth a damn, to yourself!" She then grabbed her daughter by the arm and angrily marched away from the school.

Ms. Peters went to the school principal's office to report the incident to him and solicit his guidance in helping Faith with her physical, learning, and social development problems; but instead of discussing the matter with her and trying to help resolve the problem, the principal immediately became indignant and defensive.

His response to Ms. Peters was, "What's so wrong with the child being a little overweight, Ms. Peters? Are you a doctor? No, you're sure as hell not and that's a matter for the child's mother and her doctor to deal with. Your job is only to teach, so you just stay the hell out of it and keep your judgmental attitude towards large people to yourself if you want to keep your teaching job." The principal weighed over three hundred pounds!

One kindly and caring pediatrician who examined Faith in greater depth ordered a detailed analysis of her gastrointestinal tract, and the MRI revealed that she had a disproportionately enlarged stomach and problems with her intestinal system.

He suggested to Rebecca that Faith be placed on a special stringent diet along with taking some new medications, and consider having a surgical procedure done to reduce the size of her stomach and correct her intestinal problems. The doctor also suggested to Rebecca that she should consider having the same procedure done for herself to treat her obvious and rapidly growing obesity.

Instead of appreciating the doctor's professionally sound and well intended recommendations, Rebecca took them as personal insults and angrily snapped back at him. "What you're suggesting we do is a mean and stupid idea that you came up with just to hurt me and my child's feelings, and make more money for yourself. There isn't anything wrong with my child and me, and you're nothing but a damned rotten, selfish quack to recommend that we do something so painful and expensive."

She continued to verbally attack him with several more crude expletives and the now offended kindly doctor became angry and suggested that she and her daughter should consider going to a church to help clean up her foul mouth. Rebecca jumped up from her chair, gave the doctor the middle finger, and shouted at him, "You go straight to hell, you rotten son of a bitch," then angrily slammed out of his office.

Rebecca was so enraged over the doctor's suggestions that she ceased trying to obtain any further medical help from him for Faith or herself, and vowed to get even with him. Out of revenge, she filed a complaint against the well-meaning doctor with the Hospital Administrator and the State Medical Board, claiming that he had personally insulted her and her child by trying to get them to do something inappropriate for his own selfish benefit, and she even falsely accused him of trying to force her into inappropriate sexual activity.

Based on Rebecca's complaint, the State Medical Board issued a temporary suspension of the doctor's medical license while Rebecca's charges were being investigated. News of his suspension leaked out and quickly spread around town.

The caring doctor became so depressed over this humiliating and unjust blemish on his otherwise long-term perfect professional record, and his status as a leader in his church and the community, that he committed suicide.

When she learned of his suicide, Rebecca's only comment about it was, "The cruel bastard damned well got what he deserved for wanting to treat my daughter and me the mean way that he tried to."

\*\*\*

Janice had become a disillusioned and depressed young woman. When her second child, a little girl, was born, she had no one to rely upon for help with her baby daughter except her nine-year-old son, Wallace. Her relationship with her husband had become limited to occasional drinking and partying, and his relationship with either of their children was almost non-existent. Being so lonely and becomingly increasingly obese, she was willing to accept this small and pathetic aspect of her relationship with her husband.

Despite the cash appearing in Bert's pockets every night to purchase alcohol and drugs, he never deemed it necessary to pay the family's bills, so Janice had to take a job cleaning homes for "under the table" money in order to put food on the table for her children. Bert finally disappeared from the home with a younger woman he had met in a bar one night, and was never heard from again.

Although she was pregnant with her third child, Janice was able to find a regular paying job as a clerk at a convenience store in the nearby Fayetteville suburb of Hope Mills, and moved her children and herself to a small government subsidized apartment within walking distance of the store. After the delivery of her last baby, a little boy, the State of North Carolina gladly arranged for Janice to have her ovarian tubes tied.

The family's relocation put young Wallace in a different school district; however, Janice never bothered to register him there because she needed him to take care of the toddler and infant while she worked, so he fell out of the system and never returned to school after the sixth grade.

Wallace's only recreation during the time he was caring for his siblings while his mother worked was in his prolific reading. He was a naturally well-built and handsome young boy, but his only physical activity had essentially become limited to keeping their apartment clean and taking care of his little siblings.

During lulls from acting as the man of the home, he would stretch out on the sofa and devour his books. The bookmobile of the Fayetteville Public Library came by the public housing apartment complex every Monday, and Wallace never missed an opportunity to search through the offerings and load up on topics that interested him.

As the two younger children grew older, Wallace taught them more and more how to look out for themselves, always ensuring that they were safe and responsible. As he neared his eighteenth birthday, Wallace took and easily passed the GED examination and then, on the day he turned eighteen, walked five miles to the military recruiting office in downtown Fayetteville and joined the Army.

Wallace's military service started out quite well, and he was the top graduate in his basic training class at Fort Leonard Wood, MO. After receiving additional training at Fort Jackson, SC to become an infantry soldier, he was assigned to the 82nd Airborne Division at Fort Bragg, located close to his home town of Fayetteville, and things were beginning to look up for him.

Shortly after arriving at Fort Bragg, Wallace visited with his beloved mother and siblings, but then had to leave for Fort Benning, Georgia a week later for a little over a month of basic airborne training.

On the day after he left for Fort Benning, his mother, who had grown morbidly obese from her over consumption of fattening food and alcohol, suffered an alcohol-induced stroke and spent three days in the hospital before she finally died. Wallace had just reported for training at Fort Benning and was never told of his mother's death.

When he returned to Fayetteville from Fort Benning, Wallace tried to telephone his mother but was advised that the phone number he dialed was no longer in service. He then went to her apartment where he learned from a neighbor that she had died a month before.

He was also told by the neighbor that his two younger siblings, a sister and a brother, had been placed into foster care by the Department of Social Services and had been adopted immediately after their mother's death.

When he called and spoke to the Social Services caseworker who handled his siblings' case, Wallace was told that they had been adopted by an out-of-town family and he wasn't allowed to have any further information about or contact with them at the request of the adoptive parents.

Frustrated and angry, Wally further investigated and determined that his Company First Sergeant had been given the information about his mother being hospitalized by his Company Commander, who directed him to contact Wallace while he was at Fort Benning and make arrangements for Wallace to come home on emergency leave; but the First Sergeant claimed he had been too busy at the time and had forgotten to do so.

Upon learning of this, Wallace went into a rage and physically attacked his First Sergeant, beating him so badly that he had to be hospitalized; then, after beating up his First Sergeant, Wallace went downtown and spent most of the day drinking beer and became totally drunk.

In his drunken state, Wallace went to the Department of Social Services building in Fayetteville, where he was arrested by the police for shouting a threat to kill the caseworker if she didn't let him know the whereabouts of his siblings.

These offenses resulted in Wallace spending a month in jail, having a permanent restraining order issued by the Court that directed him to cease in his efforts to contact his siblings, and he was subsequently dismissed from the Army with an undesirable discharge.

After he was put out of the Army, the only employment Wallace was able to find was a part-time, minimum paying job helping to slaughter hogs at the Smithfield

Packing Plant near Tar Heel, NC. But he was fired shortly afterwards when he was caught drinking on the job and, like his father, Wallace then turned to petty crime as a means of supporting himself.

# Chapter Three

By the time Faith was ten years of age, she weighed over one hundred pounds, puffed and waddled when she walked, and would become angrily defiant towards nearly everyone she met. In her angry and depressed state of mind, she assumed that everyone she encountered would view her as some kind of an ugly, fat freak, and this caused her to become even angrier, more obese, and more asocial.

The only constant interest in Faith's life had become food, food, and more food...especially sweet and fattening foods. She had no playmates, hobbies, or other normal childhood interests, and her mother was like her. In addition to her poor eating habits and sedentary lifestyle, Rebecca had become heavily addicted to alcohol and tobacco, and was consuming a twelve-pack of beer and two packs of cigarettes per day.

Late one night while Faith was asleep, Rebecca suffered a massive heart attack. The following morning, Faith found her mother lying on the bathroom floor, cold, unresponsive, and with her eyes frozen wide open. After unsuccessfully trying to awaken her mother, Faith desperately ran to a neighbor and cried for help. The neighbor called 911 and, when the ambulance arrived at the trailer park, Rebecca was declared dead.

A crying, confused, and frightened Faith was then taken from her home by agents of the Cumberland County Child Protective Services and placed in a foster home under the care of foster parents, Mike and Sonya Odom, a kindly childless couple in their forties.

As one of the Child Protective Service's favorite go-to volunteer couples, Mike, a retired senior Army noncommissioned officer, and Sonya, a successful businesswoman, had gladly provided temporary care for many abused and orphaned children in their home over the years. The tenure with the children in their temporary care usually lasted six months or more until they were adopted; however, the ordinarily patient and loving couple was ready to give up on Faith after having her in their home for only one week.

As a result of their troubling experience with Faith, the Odom's were so disheartened that they chose to immediately cease serving in the foster parent program to which they had been so deeply committed for the past ten years, and redirected their loving care giving to the many horses and dogs on their beautiful rural farm outside of Fayetteville.

Faith was then passed around from one foster family to another and, by the time she was twelve, she had lived briefly with nine different families. She was finally considered to be unadoptable and placed in the Cumberland County Orphanage on the outskirts of Fayetteville where she was scheduled by the Department of Social Services to stay for the remainder of her childhood.

Her adjustment to the orphanage environment was similar to that of her adjustment to foster care, school, and everything else in her young life...very poor! She was frequently disciplined for failing to comply with the orphanage's rules, and most of her violations had to do with trying to satisfy her voracious appetite when she was caught stealing extra food from the orphanage's kitchen on several occasions or for her defiant anger towards people in general.

By the time she was fourteen years old and ready to start high school, Faith weighed nearly two hundred pounds, had developed type two adult onset diabetes, and had her first menstrual period which, as with virtually everything else in her sad life, was yet another embarrassing disaster.

She hadn't been told what was happening to her body, and the poor child attributed the menstrual bleeding to her being overweight, which seemed to be the case with most of her other problems.

Out of embarrassment and desperation, she duct taped a wash cloth and plastic bag between her legs in a pathetic effort to try and control the problem, and kept it on until two days later when the orphanage's visiting nurse was able to treat the infected irritation that had occurred between her heavy legs and educate her on this issue.

Faith would often stare through teary eyes at the heavy globs of fat that were hanging down from her stomach and thighs, and become irrationally angry with her body to the point that she began cutting on the fattest areas of her skin with a razor blade.

On several occasions, she even seriously considered suicide as a way out of her miserable life but, recalling what had happened to her father in his failed suicide attempt, the idea never went to the next level of planning or actual attempting it.

When she felt severely depressed, which was the majority of the time; she would just eat more, especially sweet and fattening food, to help ease her emotional pain. Although she hated everything about her body, she continued to feed her addiction with more of the unhealthiest kinds of foods and maintained a sedentary lifestyle, which only made her grow even larger, unhealthier, and more depressed.

The first eight years of school had been a nearly constant nightmare for Faith and she dreaded going to the ninth grade even more; but she knew she had no other choice but to remain in high school until she reached the age of sixteen and could legally drop out.

\*\*\*

When Faith was driven by the orphanage bus for her first day at Fayetteville's Terry Sanford High School, she was filled with anxiety over being in the presence of this new group of older children.

From her past experience, she assumed that she would be ridiculed about her size, and her worst fears were quickly realized as she waddled down the school hallway amidst snickering, whispering, and being pointing at by the other students. She knew to whom they were directing their cruel and pain-causing attention...to the ugly fat girl herself!

She was directed to meet with Cheryl Peters, a divorced mother of two very successful children, who would be her school counselor. Cheryl was the same teacher who had once tried to help Faith when she was in the third grade, and was nearly fired by the also obese principal of the school for expressing her concern about Faith's obesity. Cheryl had since earned her Master's degree in counseling and was now serving as a counselor of students at the high school.

When Faith walked into Ms. Peters' office, Cheryl immediately recognized her from their previous relationship and warmly greeted her like a long-lost relative. As a smiling Cheryl hugged her she said, "I'm so happy to see you again, Faith, and I know you're going to just love it here and you'll do a lot of fun and rewarding things while you're a high school student."

Faith said nothing in reply, but only shrugged her shoulders and stared away with a sad frown on her unhappy face.

"Well how is your mother doing, Faith?" Ms. Peters cheerfully asked.

"My stupid mother died almost five years ago, Ms. Peters, and she's a lot better off being dead since she had gotten so fat and ugly, just like I am," replied a long-faced and obviously very angry Faith.

"I'm so sorry to hear that, Honey; then where are you living now?" Cheryl asked.

"I'm staying over at the County Children's Home. It's a stinking orphanage and I hate being there just like I know I'm gonna hate being here, too."

Cheryl gently placed her arm around Faith's shoulder, looked directly into her eyes, and said, "Honey, please try to not look at school in such a negative way because you and I are going to work together while you're here to help ensure that it will be one of the best experiences of your life.

There are so many exciting things for you to do and learn while you're in high school, and having a positive attitude towards this new adventure in your life will make it a much more enjoyable and rewarding experience for you."

Faith stared hard into Cheryl's face and said, "Look, Ms. Peters, I feel like you mean well by what you're saying to me, just like I guess you did before when I was little - I mean younger - 'cause I've never been little; but I'm so fat and ugly that I just hate being around people.

I know the other kids here are gonna treat me like

they did when I was in grammar and middle school by teasing me and making me cry, and make me hate myself for being so fat, dumb and ugly."

Cheryl looked straight into Faith's eyes and replied, "Listen carefully to me Faith; you are neither ugly nor dumb. In fact, you are actually a basically very beautiful and intelligent young lady, but I'm sure you realize that taking off a little bit of weight would help to enhance your appearance, make you healthier, and make you feel a lot better about yourself.

Would you like me to try and get you some help in doing something about your weight, Faith? I know some really good and caring professional people in town who might be able to help you feel and look better. If you're interested, I'll be glad to put you in touch with one of them."

Faith began to weep, and Cheryl again put her arms around Faith's wide body in an effort to comfort her. She suddenly pulled away from her counselor and screamed at her, "Damn you, Ms. Peters; you really do hate me, too, just like everybody else does because I'm fat, dumb and ugly, don't you?"

Cheryl calmly replied, "No, honey, I don't hate you at all and I wish you would stop saying that you're ugly and dumb, because you're not. As I've told you many times before, you're actually a very beautiful and intelligent young lady and I really do love and care about you like I do about all of my students.

I know you're going to be a good girl while you're here, and I'll be available for you anytime you want to talk with me. Would you like to take some lunch time walks with me for your first few days so we can talk about how things are going for you?"

Faith coldly declined Cheryl's kind invitation on the grounds that she couldn't miss her lunchtime because of her diabetic condition and need for food, and angrily stomped out of Cheryl's office.

\*\*\*

When she reported to her homeroom, Faith was filled with even more anxiety over the way she expected she would be treated by the other kids. One of her classmates who had been with her the previous year in the eighth grade recognized Faith and attempted to greet her. Faith snubbed her classmate's greeting, quickly turned away from the girl with an angry scowl on her face, and slumped down in a seat at the very rear of the classroom.

Her attractive and physically fit young homeroom teacher, Miss Ploeger, cheerfully greeted the class. "Welcome to Terry Sanford High School, you wonderful young people! I'm so glad to see you all and I'm looking forward to our working together during your first year as you prepare to achieve your educational goals in life.

I'll share with you a little about the personal experiences that I had when I was where you are in my own life, and then I would like for each of you to share a little about yourself.

My sister, Suzanne, and I both attended and graduated from this same school several years ago, where we played on the girls' soccer team, sang in the school glee club, and had four absolutely wonderful years here.

I then attended North Carolina State University, where I received my bachelor's and master's degrees in Secondary Education. Suzanne graduated from the University of North Carolina with a bachelor's degree in biology, and is now in medical school at Ohio State University, where she is studying to become a pediatric physician.

Like I'm sure many of you may be feeling right now,

we were both also having a little anxiety over this new experience in our lives at the beginning; but we soon discovered that maintaining a steady commitment to our goals and lots of hard work would pay off big, and they certainly have done that for us.

I know all of you will have a similarly rewarding experience while you're here at Terry Sanford High School as well, if you keep a positive attitude towards your schoolwork and stay focused on your priorities in life. Now, I'd like for each of you to introduce yourself and briefly share with me and the other members of your class what you hope to accomplish in your life while you're here."

The first student, Bianca, an attractive young girl whose parents were from India, stood and said, "Although it's a little scary for me right now, m'am, like you said it was for you and your sister at the beginning, I'm really very excited to finally be a high school student.

I like to play tennis and hope that one day I'll be good enough at it to play on our school's tennis team, and I also like to paint and draw and would like to take art lessons. After I graduate from high school, I'm planning on going on to college and maybe even go on to medical school and become a doctor like my father, or maybe go into the business world like my mother."

"Thank you for sharing, Bianca; that's a very nice plan you have for yourself and I wish you the very best in making all your dreams come true. How about you, Faith? What are your initial thoughts about being in high school and what are your plans for your future?"

Faith pouted as she sat with her head down and arms tightly crossed and said nothing. Miss Ploeger again asked in a raised voice, "Faith please tell us a little about yourself and what you hope to accomplish while you're a student here at Terry Sanford High School."

Faith slowly stood up from her desk with a scowl and tears flowing down her face and indignantly shouted, "I don't have any plans for my screwed up life except to get even fatter and uglier than I already am, and drop out of this damned stupid school as soon as I turn sixteen," and then she angrily slumped back down into her chair and whimpered. This behavior brought on a surge of laughter from the other students.

Shocked, Miss Ploeger didn't know how to respond to Faith's vituperative outburst, so she ignored it and immediately went on to the next child while the rest of the class continued to giggle over Faith's pathetic and angry response.

As she went to each of her classes, Faith would walk alone with her head hung low and stare at her feet. She couldn't wait for the horrible first day of high school to be over.

As she passed the other girls and boys in the hallway who were having fun chatting and laughing with one another, she so desperately longed to have friends who would like and accept her as she was; but she had sadly learned from her past experiences that this would probably never happen in her life.

Since her first day of kindergarten, Faith had never experienced a single happy moment in school, with each day being a struggle for survival from her peers' criticism and teasing, and a constant craving for more candy and other fattening food.

\*\*\*

When her very unhappy first day of high school had finally ended and she was back at the orphanage, Faith immediately rushed up to her room and opened the large stash of candy bars that she kept hidden in a laundry bag, and which she frequently used to treat her chronic hunger and depression. As she was devouring her second large Butterfinger candy bar, Kathy Lewis, a petite orphanage staff member, entered Faith's room.

"Where did you get all of that candy, Faith?" Kathy sternly asked. "You know it's a violation of the orphanage's rules for you to keep such things in your room. That is exactly the kind of a thing that has kept you in constant trouble ever since you got here and also why you've gotten to be so fat and sick with diabetes. I'm going to take all of this candy to the director's office and submit a rule violation report about it." She then reached out to take the remaining candy bars away from Faith.

Faith, who weighed nearly twice as much as Kathy, screamed back at her, "You better leave my stuff the hell alone, you mean, nosey little bitch," kicked her in the shins, shoved her down onto the floor, and retrieved the candy. Kathy screamed for help and within a few minutes two other staff members came rushing to her aid. They placed Faith into restraints and led her to the orphanage director's office, kicking, cursing, and screaming all the way.

As Faith sat sobbing in the office, the orphanage's director, Elizabeth Sasser, firmly advised her that this was her final chance to avoid being transferred to a state facility for unmanageable children, and that the next violation of the orphanage's rules of conduct would give her no choice but to dismiss her from the orphanage and have her transferred. There had been many violations by Faith before, all dealing with anger-driven insubordination towards the staff and the possession of stolen contraband food items.

Ms. Sasser told Faith, "I'm going to forgive you for your misconduct for the very last time and give you one final chance to stay here at the orphanage, Faith, because I do like you and want you to turn your life around and be a happy and successful girl. But if there's another incident like this one, you will leave me no choice but to send you away to the state school. Do you understand me, young lady?"

Faith knew this transfer would be even worse for her, food accessibility and discipline-wise, and expressed an insincere remorseful apology to Ms. Sasser for what she had done. "Yes m'am, I do understand that what I did was wrong, and I'm very sorry. Thank you for giving me another chance, Ms. Sasser, and I promise you that I'll be nicer and will never do anything bad like that again if you don't send me away."

Later that night, after the rest of the children were asleep, Faith quietly slipped down to the orphanage's kitchen and opened the refrigerator. Inside, she found half of a chocolate pie and she quickly scooped it up with her hands, stuffing the gooey chocolate filling into her mouth, and then hurried back to her room with chocolate spread over her hands and face.

# Chapter Four

Early the next morning, Faith slowly crawled out of bed, dressed, and got herself ready for another dreaded bus ride to Terry Sanford High School. When she arrived at the school, the reception from some of her classmates was even worse than it had been on her first day, because they now knew her name and the word about her outburst on the day before had gotten around. The hurtful ridiculing that commenced was now even more personalized and painful.

When she walked into her homeroom, Ms. Ploeger told her that Mrs. Peters wanted to see her in her office right away.

When she arrived at Ms. Peters' office, she saw a well-dressed and distinguished-looking, middle-aged man sitting in the office with her. "Good morning, Faith. I have someone I'd like you to meet. Dr. John Chambers, this is my young friend and one of our freshman students, Faith Thomas."

Dr. Chambers gave Faith a friendly smile, rose from his chair, shook her hand, and said, "I'm so pleased to meet you, Miss Thomas."

Faith was sullenly quiet and didn't respond to Dr. Chambers' greeting. She anxiously thought, *what in the hell is this all about and who is this man?*

Ms. Peters said, "Dr. Chambers is a good friend of mine and he's a surgeon at the Cape Fear Valley Medical Center. He's such a nice doctor who has done a wonderful job in helping several of our other students who had weight problems like yours to look and feel so much better.

I know you're pretty sensitive about this matter, Faith, but I want you to know that we do understand the burden you've been carrying, and Dr. Chambers is willing to help you if you want his help. He does a special surgical procedure at his hospital to help correct young people's weight problems and the results have been absolutely amazing and fast. Would you like Dr. Chambers to help you, Faith?"

Feeling trapped and intimidated to be speaking with a doctor, especially one who cuts on people, Faith meekly replied, "I don't know, Dr. Chambers; I'll have to think about it and get back to you. I know I'm a big embarrassment to Ms. Peters and the rest of the school for being so ugly and fat like I am, but I don't know if I want to be helped if means that I'll have to be cut on."

She wanted to scream at them to leave her alone and go to hell, and immediately run away to get out of this situation, but she knew this might result in her being sent away to the dreaded state home. So she tried to tough it out by not fully expressing the anger she was feeling towards Cheryl and the doctor for what she perceived as their obvious disapproval of and intention to hurt her. She was feeling a strong craving for something sweet, like a candy bar, to help ease her anxiety.

After Faith left the office, Cheryl apologized to Dr. Chambers for Faith's rejection of his kind offer to help her.

Dr. Chambers replied, "Don't give up on her yet, Cheryl. My door will always be open for her if and when she should decide to take advantage of my help. Her rejection of my offer to help her doesn't surprise or personally offend me at all, though, because many young people who suffer from her condition are actually *afraid* to change something with which they've lived for so much of their lives and gotten adjusted to, even though their obesity is painful for them.

From my experience, I believe there's a good chance that she'll come back to you and ask for my help later, maybe even before the school year is over. Just give me a call if and when she does and I'll be glad to help her."

After Dr. Chambers left, Cheryl went to the principal's office to speak with him about Faith. After hearing the whole story, the principal commended Cheryl for her dedication by having gone well above and beyond her professional responsibilities in trying to help Faith, and assured her of his full support in helping this poor child to get on the right track.

***

Faith deeply dreaded her first physical education class. She knew she would be required to wear a tee shirt, shorts, and tennis shoes, and this would only expose more of her fat body and probably bring on even more teasing and hurtful humiliation from her classmates. When she entered the girls' locker room, she was extremely anxious, and was dreading to have to change her clothes in front of the other girls.

Her fears were quickly realized when she tried to slip into a remote corner of the locker room so as to be as far away as possible from the other girls when she removed her clothes. When she took off her pants and the huge globules of fat on her buttocks, thighs, and belly with scabs from the self-inflicted cuts were exposed, the entire room full of girls suddenly gathered around Faith and roared in laughter, which caused Faith to break into heavy tears.

She jumped up, screamed expletives at them, shot them a middle finger; then struggled to put on her gym clothes, and angrily followed the group of girls into the gymnasium.

As her physical education teacher was leading the girls through stretching and light warm-up drills, poor Faith huffed and puffed hard as she tried her best to keep up with them. Then, when the class was led outdoors for a short one-quarter mile jog around the school track, she collapsed onto the ground, exhausted and crying, just moments after beginning the run.

She was taken to the school nurse, Sharon McManus, R.N., who determined that Faith's collapse was due to her excessive weight and a hypoglycemic reaction to her diabetes. Mrs. McManus arranged with Cheryl and the physical education teacher to set up a special individual physical fitness program for Faith; one where she would be allowed to exercise alone so she could develop at her own pace and not have to suffer any more embarrassment from doing exercises with her peers.

At the end of her first miserable week of high school, Faith had about decided that she just couldn't take any more of the stressors of her current life, leaving her with no other choice but to either run away from both the school and the orphanage or kill herself.

Recalling her father's failed attempt to commit suicide, she was afraid to try killing herself and passed on that idea; and if she ran away she didn't know where she could go or what she would do. Nor did she have any idea about what new miseries might lay ahead for her, but she was determined not to stay where she was any longer, regardless of the consequences. She decided that she had to take her chances and run away from Fayetteville and the orphanage as quickly as possible.

Being as large as she was, and at an average adult female height of five-five, Faith was often mistaken for an adult, so she decided she would try to pass herself off as one and developed her escape strategy based on that.

As she began to put her escape plan together, Faith figured the first thing she needed would be some money to sustain her until she could find a job doing something - anything to get her away from the orphanage, find a safe place to stay, and be able to eat whatever and as much as she wanted.

Late that Friday night after the lights in her dormitory were turned off, Faith slipped down the hall to the room of the staff duty person, Mary Kay Adams, a graduate student from nearby Methodist University who worked at the orphanage as a part-time child caretaker, and found her napping in a chair. Mary Kay's purse was lying on a table beside her. Faith silently removed the purse from the table and then slipped quietly back to her room to examine its contents.

The purse contained sixty-eight dollars and forty-four cents in cash, a driver's license, a bank debit card, and some assorted cosmetics. Faith was pleased to note that Mary Kay had written her account pass code number on the debit card, which meant she could withdraw whatever money Mary Kay had in her bank account from an ATM at a nearby bank, and she could use Mary Kay's driver's license as an adult ID.

Faith also found an expensive looking necklace and a pair of matching earrings in the purse and figured she could wear them to look more grownup when looking for a job, or sell them to provide more money to help sustain her until...*until what?*, she thought to herself. Faith was determined that she would somehow find a job of some kind to help her get by and, most of all, to be able to have the kinds and amounts of food she wanted.

She didn't even have a clue as to where she would sleep on her first night of "freedom" but was determined to leave early the following morning, regardless of what the outcome might be. In her depressed state of mind, even being dead would seem to be a better option for her than her current life was.

\*\*\*

At a little before five a.m. on Saturday morning, Faith took the purse and a pillow case stuffed with a few of her only earthly possessions, a light jacket, a sweater, two pairs of pants, two blouses, two changes of underwear, two pairs of shoes and socks, six sanitary napkins, a hair brush, two candy bars, and some cosmetics she had found in Mary Kay's purse, and quietly slipped out the back door of the orphanage and into the piney woods.

It was a cool, damp, and breezy morning, and the sun was just beginning to break through the overcast clouds as Faith walked through the woods behind the orphanage on a small trail that would lead out to the main highway.

She had no idea where she would go or how she would survive after getting there; but knew one thing for sure... she had to get away from the misery of living in the orphanage, going to school, and virtually every aspect of her present life, and there could be no turning back now. It was either leaving the orphanage that she despised, or having to face being sent to the dreaded state facility where her life would be even worse.

When Faith arrived at the NC Route 87 South highway, she wandered along the shoulder of the road in a mental daze; frightened, tired, and not really knowing where she was heading.

A pickup truck suddenly pulled up in front of her and stopped on the shoulder of the road. The young man driving it slowly backed up, leaned his head out of the window and shouted back to her, "Hey there, girl. Can I give you a ride?"

Without giving any consideration to the potential danger of getting into the stranger's truck, Faith immediately accepted the man's offer in order to get out of the chilling wind and the light rain that was beginning to fall. Once inside his truck, the young man cheerfully asked her, "Hey girl, where are you heading so early on this miserably chilly and wet morning?"

Not knowing what to say, she mumbled to him, "I'm going to look for a job."

The young man asked, "Are you thinking about applying for work at the pork plant that's a couple of miles up the road near Tar Heel?"

Faith had heard of the Smithfield Packing Company's large pork processing plant located between Fayetteville and the small town of Tar Heel from previous hurting and teasing remarks that had been made by other children. They had jokingly advised her to stay away from it least she be mistaken for a hog, be slaughtered, and turned into a package of lunch meat.

"I'm not sure that's where I want to work, but I might give it a try," replied Faith

"Do you know which shift you want to be working on or what you want to do there?" he asked.

Faith replied, "No, I don't know anything yet because I'm just going to apply to work there today, but whatever shift they put me on or whatever I do really doesn't matter to me as long as I can get myself a paying job."

He said, "I used to work there myself right after I was

thrown out of the Army. I worked there for a few weeks as a hog butcher's helper 'til they fired me when they caught me drinking a beer on the job a couple of months ago."

Faith asked, "You keep asking me questions, so let me ask you one. What kind of work are you doing now?"

He replied with a chuckle, "I make some pretty good dough by sifting through people's trash cans and checking outside their houses late at night. I sell the good stuff that I usually find. Heck, I'm making a whole lot more money now by doing that than I ever did when I was working my ass off at a regular job, and I don't even have to pay any damned taxes on it either. By the way, girl, my name is Wallace Cochran, but all my friends call me Wally...what's yours?"

Faith hesitated and replied, "My name is Mary Kay Adams and I'm pleased to meet you, Wally." She had already rehearsed several times to memorize the name, address, and date of birth of the girl whose driver's license and ATM card she had stolen and was carrying in her purse.

"You got yourself a boy friend, Mary Kay?" Wally asked.

Without thinking, Faith impulsively blurted out, "Are you kidding me, Wally? Who in the hell would want to have a fat, ugly person like me for a girl friend?"

Wally replied, "Hey, don't put yourself down, Mary Kay. You're not ugly at all; in fact, I think you're pretty cute and being a little overweight sure as hell ain't no crime. Hell, I like to eat too, so what's wrong with that?"

Faith was beside herself! She thought, *this guy thinks I'm pretty cute; he's mighty cute, too and he's not putting me down for being fat like everybody else does. I like him a lot!*

Wally asked her, "Wanna let's stop at the convenience store down the road and grab us a cup of hot chocolate and a jelly doughnut to chill out a little before you go over to apply at the packing plant, Mary Kay?"

At that moment, Faith would probably have gone to Hell with him if Wally had asked her to. He was the first and only boy in her entire life to ever speak directly and kindly to her and to tell her she was pretty cute had Faith floating on a cloud of delirious joy. She said, "That would be real nice, Wally, and I'd like to do that."

Wally and Faith sat across from each other at a picnic table outside a convenience store in the small town of Tar Heel, just about a mile south of the packing plant. Faith's thighs and buttocks were so large that she could barely sit comfortably on the small wooden bench.

Wally brought two large cups of hot chocolate and two jelly doughnuts over to the table for them. Faith added four heaping teaspoons of sugar to her cup of hot chocolate, began to gulp it down, and then quickly gobbled up the jelly doughnut that tasted so good and helped to calm her nerves.

They chatted for a short while longer; then Wally asked, "Mary Kay, how would you like to go over to my place for awhile? It's not far from here and you can warm up and get yourself ready to go over to the plant's human resource department that's only a few minutes away. They're not gonna be open until after nine o'clock, and that's over two hours from now."

Although it made her feel a little uneasy, she accepted Wally's invitation to stop over at his place, and away they went. As they were riding, an Amber Alert was broadcast over the radio. Faith quickly turned the dial to another station before a full description of the missing child could be reported, and she told Wally that she'd prefer listening to some good music than hearing the boring news if he didn't mind.

A few minutes later they pulled into a run-down and

small trailer park, and stopped beside a little singlewide camping trailer. Wally said, "Well, we're home now, Mary Kay, so welcome to my humble little castle!"

They got out of Wally's pickup truck and went into the small, dirty, and much disarrayed trailer. They had barely gotten inside when Wally suddenly pulled Faith close to him and gave her a long and lingering wet kiss, the very first kiss Faith had ever received from a boy, and she enthusiastically returned it. It was intoxicating to her!

One thing then quickly led to another and Faith was soon naked and lying in the bed, with Wally on top of her. When he entered her, it was a mixture of an emotionally great feeling of being wanted and cared for by this seemingly wonderful and handsome boy, along with a little bit of initial physical discomfort when her hymen was penetrated.

She knew what she was allowing him to do to her by taking away her virginity and possibly impregnating her was wrong, but she was so ecstatic over Wally's attention and seeming caring for her that she gladly allowed him to have his way with her, regardless of the consequences.

After what was an exhilarating experience for Faith and they were lying together and relaxing on Wally's small bed, he looked at his watch and told her it was nearly nine o'clock and asked if she wanted to get dressed and ready to head on over to the packing plant's human resource office.

She yawned and said, "I don't know, Wally. I feel so relaxed and comfortable just lying right here for now. Would it be okay with you if I stay over with you here in your place tonight and go over to the plant early tomorrow morning instead after the hard rain stops?"

To her satisfaction and comfort, Wally replied, "Sure, baby, we'll do whatever you want...whatever makes you happy will make me happy too." They both then fell into a deep and relaxing sleep for the remainder of the morning.

When Faith finally awakened early that afternoon, Wally was standing over her with his arms crossed and he sternly asked her, "Okay gal, just who the hell are you...I mean what is your *real* name?"

Faith replied, "I told you before, Wally, my name is Mary Kay Adams. Why are you asking me that again?"

Frowning, he sternly said, "There's no way in hell that you're Mary Kay Adams, girl, so why don't you just tell me the damned truth, whoever you are? You really don't need to lie to me anymore."

Faith wondered, *why is he asking me that and what does he know?* Then she looked over and saw her purse was lying open on the table and she knew...he must have looked at Mary Kay's driver's license!

Wally continued, "Look, whoever you are, I'm not trying to give you a hard time about it, but I just want to know what the truth is, so don't give me any more bullshit, okay? Don't get mad at me for doing it, but my curiosity got to me so I decided to check out your purse while you were sleeping.

I looked at Mary Kay's driver's license and you don't even look anything at all like her picture. She's just five feet tall, redheaded, and weighs only a hundred and five pounds, so why don't you shoot straight with me girl? You have blonde hair and I know you weigh a helluva lot more than a hundred and five pounds. I promise I won't be mad at you if you just tell me the damned truth, whoever you are."

Faith was alarmed with fear. *If I tell him who I really am, will he turn me in to the police? If he does, they may send me away to the State School or maybe even put me in jail for stealing Mary Kay Adams' purse. Oh hell, I better take a chance and tell him the truth and hope he won't throw me out or turn me in!*

She began to weep and said, "Okay, Wally, you're right; I'm really not Mary Kay. My real name is Faith Thomas and I ran away from an orphanage that I hated early this morning just before you picked me up. I took Mary Kay's things and know what I did was wrong, but please don't turn me over to the cops; because if you do they'll make me go to jail or live in a place that I know I'll hate even worse than I did living at the orphanage.

Please, Wally, let me stay here with you for just a little while longer where I feel safe and comfortable, and I promise you I'll leave first thing tomorrow morning."

Wally gave her a warm hug and said, "Don't you worry your sweet self, honey. I understand your situation and I don't care much for the cops either. I'll be glad to help you out if you want me to."

Through sobbing tears, Faith then told Wally more about her whole life's situation. When she finished telling him her story, they hugged, and he expressed his sympathy for what she had been experiencing because he had gone through a tough growing up in his life as well.

He said, "You're welcome to stay here with me for awhile until after the heat is over and they stop looking for you, or for as long as you want to stay. I'll take care of you, Faith; in fact, you can even work with me for awhile in my little business if you want to because I could use a partner to keep a lookout for the cops when I go out at night to pick up stuff to sell."

Faith was beside herself with the happiest feelings she'd ever experienced in her entire life! This kindly and good-looking boy not only liked her, they had made love together for the first time in her life, he was going to help her by giving her a job working with him, and said he would also take care of her. She felt so safe and secure with Wally that, in her irrational, immature, and euphoric state of mind, she even fantasized about the two of them getting married one day soon.

Wally told her he had also seen Mary Kay's ATM card in her purse and suggested that they head over to the bank as soon as possible to see what they might be able to get from it before Mary Kay reported it as stolen.

They drove to a nearby branch of the First Citizens' Bank with Faith wearing a ski cap and a pair of dark glasses Wally had given her to serve as a disguise when the bank's security camera would videotape her while she was using Mary Kay's card to make a cash withdrawal.

Faith slipped the debit card into the ATM and punched in the pass code numbers Mary Kay had written on the card. When it opened the account, at Wally's direction, Faith punched in the withdrawal amount of two hundred dollars. After a brief pause, the machine spat out ten twenty-dollar bills!

Wally said, "Let's try it again, honey, and see if it'll give us some more dough."

They did it again and again. By the time the ATM stopped spitting out any more money, they had gotten six hundred dollars and were elated!

On their way back to Wally's trailer, they stopped by the Food Lion grocery store where they bought two shopping carts filled with some food, along with a large package of Twinkies, a box of candy bars, and a quart bottle of Mountain Dew for Faith; and a case of beer and a carton of cigarettes for Wally.

While Faith was busily putting away their groceries and straightening up the trailer, there was a knock on the trailer door and Wally answered it. It was a friend of Wally's, Billy Joe Martin, who was also one of Wally's main fences for stolen goods.

Billy Joe stood in the door and asked, "Hey, man, I hope I'm not interrupting anything with you two, am I? You got some good stuff to sell me today, Wally?"

Wally replied, "Yeah, man, not a problem...come on in. I've got some pretty good stuff outside in my truck that I picked up last night, including a nearly brand new lawn mower and a cool children's bicycle. I'll be right out in a second to show everything to you. By the way, Billy Joe, this here's my new girl friend, Faith."

*His girl friend?* Faith thought. This brought on another surge of euphoria into her pathetic mind!

While Wally and Billy Joe stood outside next to his truck looking over the stolen goods and talking, Faith's curiosity about the situation motivated her to surreptitiously eavesdrop on their conversation from a slightly opened window of the trailer.

Billy Joe asked Wally, "Where the hell did you get the big fat chick that's in there with you, man? You really do go for the fat ones don't you?" Man, I can't understand why you do that when there're plenty of good looking ones around."

Wally replied, "Yeah, you may think I'm crazy as hell for it, man, but all of the fat chicks I've been with are always grateful for the attention I give them and will do just about anything I ask them to...and this one is real special."

Although she wasn't pleased with the first part of Wally's comment to Billy Joe about referring to her as a 'fat chick', Faith was pleased to at least hear that he viewed her as *real special.*

"What the heck makes her so special, Wally?" asked Billy Joe. "I believe she's the fattest one I've ever seen you with...man, she looks like a phrigging walrus!"

Wally grinned as he pulled out a wad of twenty-dollar bills from his pocket and flashed them at his friend.

"Yeah man, I know she really is a fat one, just about the fattest one I've ever had, but she not only screws pretty good for a fat bitch, she got me this nice wad of dough to boot."

"No shit, man; where did she get it from?" asked Billy Joe.

Wally replied, "The fat bitch stole an ATM card from a friend of hers and we used it to buy a bunch of stuff and fill up my pockets with this cash."

Faith's heart pounded with sadness and anxiety over hearing Wally's remarks about her, especially about his constantly referring to her as a fat bitch, and it hurt her even worse than ever to hear that which followed.

"Well, what're you gonna do when you're through with her, man? You're surely not going to keep her here with you much longer are you?" asked Billy Joe.

Wally replied, "Hell no, man; I'm not that crazy. I'm gonna dump the fat bitch as soon as I can...maybe I'll even do it tomorrow after I screw her one more time. You can have a shot at her, yourself, if you want to, because she's not too bad in bed."

"No thanks, man; I don't dig the fat chicks like you do. What're you gonna do about it if she won't leave, Wally?" Billy Joe asked.

Wally shrugged his shoulders and laughingly said, "Hell, man, if I can't get her to leave on her own in a day or so, I might report her to the cops and let them take her away; or if that doesn't work, I might even have to kill the bitch and dump her fat ass in the river and let the fish have a feast on her."

Faith began to sob hysterically. Only a few minutes ago, she had felt so protected, cared for, and loved by Wally, and was the happiest she had ever been; but she was suddenly now at the very lowest point of her miserable young life and her heart was completely crushed. She wasn't just saddened to hear Wally's statement about planning to kill her; she was also madder than a wet hen and nearly scared to death!

After his buddy had left, Wally headed back to the trailer where Faith was waiting for him behind the door with a large cast iron frying pan raised over her head.

As soon as he entered the trailer, she smashed Wally on the top of his head with the frying pan as hard as she could. He immediately fell to the floor unconscious, with his head severely bleeding. She continued to strike him in the head with the pan several times, causing him to bleed more while she cried, "You dirty, no-good son of a bitch, you've hurt me so bad that I hope I kill you!"

Vowing to herself that she would never trust another man again, Faith put on her jacket, threw her few things in a bag, removed the money from Wally's pockets and put it in her purse, and then headed out of the trailer door with tears streaming down her face.

# Chapter Five

Faith ran out of the trailer park and into a windy and drizzling rain with the bag containing her few belongings, including a box of candy bars they had bought earlier that day in hand and a little over three hundred of the remaining stolen dollars tucked in her purse.

When she reached the main highway, it was beginning to turn dark and she didn't know which direction she should take, north or south. As she stood shaking at the edge of the highway, she seriously thought about just jumping out in front of a fast moving truck and bringing a quick end to her miserable life, but only the fear of failing to succeed, as her father once had, kept her from doing it.

Going north meant heading back to Fayetteville, where she knew she would surely be caught and be in deeper trouble, especially if she had killed Wally - something of which she wasn't sure - and heading south meant going towards Wilmington, a town where she had never been before and didn't know anyone. After giving it a few moments of thought, she finally opted to take her chances and head south for Wilmington with the hope of being able to survive there.

She had been walking along the shoulder of the road in

the increasing darkness and rain for almost a half-mile, wondering if she had killed Wally, when a woman who was driving an old, nearly worn out station wagon whose rear end was covered with religious bumper stickers and had a plastic replica of Jesus on its dashboard pulled to a stop; then backed up and offered her a ride. The rain was beginning to come down harder, so Faith took a chance and accepted the woman's offer in order to get out of the miserable weather.

The driver, an elderly black lady, said in a kindly voice, "Get your sweet self in this car right now, child, before you get run over by a truck or drown from all this rain. Where in the world are you going all by yourself on this dark and rainy evening?"

"I'm going to Wilmington," replied Faith.

"Do you live in Wilmington?" the old lady asked.

Faith lied and said, "No m'am, I'm going there to stay with some of my kinfolks who live there."

The old lady replied, "Oh, and where do your kinfolks live in Wilmington? I'm going there too, and I'll be glad to drop you off at their house."

Feeling trapped in her lie, since she didn't even know the name of a street in Wilmington, Faith quickly thought of a street name and replied, "They live in a house on Main Street."

"Oh, I don't think I ever heard of a Main Street in Wilmington, but don't you worry; I'll find out where it is and get you there, child. Tell me, child, what are you doing all by yourself and out at nighttime in this terribly bad weather?"

Faith replied, "I just had a bad argument with some mean people I was staying with back near Tar Heel and I had to run away because one of them said he was going to hurt me."

"Your poor child, you're way too young to be having

that kind of crazy stuff happening in your life. Do you want me to stop up the road and call the police for you?"

"No, m'am, please don't do that. I'll be all right." This scared Faith because the police were the last people she wanted to see at this point, especially if she had killed Wally.

As they rode, the old lady then softly asked Faith, "Child, have you met Jesus yet?"

Faith replied, "No, m'am, I don't think I've ever met anybody by that name. Who is that?"

"Good gracious, child, don't you know that He is our Lord and Savior? Didn't your mama and daddy take you to church and Sunday school when you were a little girl?"

Faith was confused and said, "No, m'am, I've never been inside a church before, although I've heard lots of nice things about them from other people. My mama and daddy died when I was little and they never took me to a church."

She thought to herself, *Jesus? He? I sure as hell don't need another 'he' to hurt me after all I've been through with all the other he's in my life! My daddy left my mother and me when I was a child, a male doctor at the school was gonna cut me up, and then that bastard, Wally, raped me and was gonna let his buddy use me and then kill me...no, there ain't no way that I'll ever trust another damned man in my life again, period!*

Most of the remaining ninety-mile ride was spent in listening to religious music and preaching on the radio, along with the old lady explaining to Faith all about this great man called Jesus, who would save her from all harm and make her life such a happy and meaningful one.

Faith finally asked her, "M'am, where does this

wonderful person you've been talking to me about live, this man you call Jesus? Does He live over in Wilmington, too?"

The old lady replied, "Honey, our precious Jesus lives everywhere, and especially right here in my old heart. If you go to my church with me tomorrow and let me introduce you to Him, I promise you He is sure gonna make a huge difference in your young life if you'll just let Him come into your heart. If you want me to, I'll be glad to pick you up at your kinfolk's house first thing in the morning and take you to my church with me."

As they were riding and the old lady was listening to her religious music on the radio and continuing to tell her about Jesus, the program was suddenly interrupted with a news bulletin.

*A twenty-year-old man was just found bleeding and unconscious in his mobile home near the small town of Tar Heel tonight by a friend who said the man's girl friend had beaten and robbed him. The victim, Wallace Cochran of Tar Heel, had several warrants out for his arrest for petty larceny and an assault on a female. He was taken to the Cape Fear Valley Regional Medical Center by an ambulance, where Dr. John DeBoer, the surgeon who treated him, reported that Cochran is expected to make a complete recovery. Afterwards, Cochran will be transferred to the Cumberland County Detention Center to face charges.*

Faith was at least relieved to know she hadn't killed Wally, but realized that she was still in a lot of very serious trouble and could be caught and severely punished if she wasn't careful.

The old lady said, "I just can't imagine why anybody would do something so awfully mean by hurting one of God's creatures like that, can you?"

Faith mumbled, "No, m'am, I can't either, unless the man asked for it by being mean and was hurting her."

When they finally arrived in Wilmington, the old lady asked Faith to give her directions to her kinfolk's house. Faith then broke down in tears and confessed to her. "I don't really have any kinfolks here. I'm so sorry, m'am, but I told you a lie. I just had to get away from a real bad situation back in Tar Heel that was hurting me, and I didn't know where I was going."

The old lady was sympathetic to Faith's plight, and kindly said, "Then don't you worry your sweet self about it. You're gonna stay in my house tonight, child, whether you want to or not, because it's just too nasty a night for you to be out in this weather all alone and without a safe place to stay...and besides, you will be welcome to go with me to my church in the morning and meet our precious Lord Jesus."

Faith was too tired to argue with the old woman and glad she would at least have a safe, warm, and dry place to sleep that night, so she went with her into the small frame house. Once inside, she saw crosses, pictures of a smiling bearded man in a robe, and all sorts of other religious symbols that were hanging on the walls throughout the home, and they made her feel uneasy.

The old lady said, "I just realized that you don't even know my name, child, so let me introduce myself. My name is Mrs. Ella Mae Brown and I live here with my forty-year-old son, Jeremy.

My husband, William, who was the minister here at the Beulah A.M.E. church here in town for most of our life together, passed away last year and is now with our Lord. That boy of mine has had some problems with his head and got himself into bad trouble with the law, but I'm still trying to save him...me and Jesus."

*There she goes again with that talk about this man*

*called Jesus,* Faith thought. *I better get the hell outta here first thing in the morning or she'll start lecturing me with all that crazy Jesus talk again, and there's no telling what her whacko son might do to hurt me. But as tired as I am, I'll sleep anywhere tonight.*

The moment her head hit the pillow, Faith immediately fell into a deep sleep and slept through the night. At about nine a.m., Ella Mae Brown awakened her and said, "You better get up now and get yourself dressed, child, because we've got to be at my church in an hour. We sure don't want to be late for your first meeting with our dear Lord and Savior, Jesus."

Faith yawned and asked, "Do we really have to go to church, Mrs. Brown? I'm still so sleepy and tired, and I need to be on my way soon anyhow. Can't I meet with your friend, Jesus, some other time?"

"You gotta be on your way to where, child? Where are you gonna go when you leave here?" asked Ella Mae.

Since Faith had no answer to Mrs. Brown's question, and she sure didn't want to be left alone with Ella Mae's son, she said nothing but slowly crawled out of bed and started putting on her clothes. She realized she had no other choice but to go to church with Mrs. Brown until she could figure out what her next move would be.

When they left the home, Mrs. Brown was dressed "to the nines," wearing a large decorative flowered lavender hat with matching gloves and her beautifully covered Bible in hand. Faith did the best she could to look as decent as possible with what few clothes she had. She put on the necklace and earrings she had stolen from Mary Kay at the orphanage to look more adult and dressed up, and put on some of the makeup that she had also stolen from Mary Kay.

When they entered the church, Faith realized that she

was the only white person in the entire very attractive, large, and completely filled church.

The service began with the large and nicely attired robed choir singing several hymns as they clapped their hands and swayed back and forth to the beat of the piano music. Reverend Maurice Johnson, the pastor, then stepped up to the pulpit and began to say a lengthy prayer.

Faith couldn't understand much of what the pastor was saying, as he was speaking about some things that she had never heard before, and he frequently referred to the man called Jesus who Mrs. Brown had spoken so highly of during their ride from Tar Heel on the night before.

The entire congregation then rose and began singing the hymn, *Amazing Grace,* which Mrs. Brown had told Faith was her most favorite hymn of all. Faith just stood there with her arms at her side without knowing what to do. After the first verse of the hymn began, Mrs. Brown handed Faith an open hymn book and whispered to her, "Child, if you can read this, come on and start singing along with us. It'll make your soul feel real good."

Faith took the hymn book and started to sing along with the congregation. After the hymn was over, Mrs. Brown whispered to her, "Child, did you know you have a mighty sweet singing voice?" Faith thanked her, as it made her feel good to receive a nice and rare compliment from anyone about anything.

Unfortunately, though, feeling good for Faith had always been followed by a disappointment in her life, as it had been the previous day with Wally, so she began to feel a touch of anxiety from Mrs. Brown's compliment, fearing that some bad thing would soon follow.

The pastor then stood up behind the pulpit again and began to deliver his sermon. As he spoke, Faith felt as though he was looking at and talking directly to her, and it made her feel nervous because she didn't understand most of what he was saying. But one key part of his sermon came through loud and clear and registered heavily in Faith's troubled mind.

The pastor said, "My dear brothers and sisters, Our beloved father, God, and His dear son, our Lord and Savior, Jesus, have blessed us all with so many opportunities in our lives to be whatever we choose to be; but we have to be the ones to make up our minds about what it is that we want to be, and work towards accomplishing our goals. All along the way, we should pray every day for our Lord's help and inspiration for us to do what it takes to make what we want to be become a reality.

Too many of us just don't give any thought beyond where we are, though, and then we wonder why we never amount to anything worthwhile in our lives. We cannot change what we have been before, but with our Lord's help we can sure determine what we will be.

We should all adopt the Army's recruiting slogan that says, 'Be all you can be,' instead of being satisfied with ourselves with mediocrity when we all have the potential be so much more than we are. Now I want all of you brothers and sisters to say out loud, 'With our Lord's help, I will be all I can be!'" The congregation loudly repeated the pastor's direction several times.

Faith was so moved by what Reverend Johnson had said because it perfectly described her situation, especially that of needing to envision a positive and happy future aspiration for herself, so she wrote the words, "With our Lord's help, I will be all I can be" on a pew envelope and slipped the envelope into her pants pocket.

When the collection plate was passed, Faith reached into her purse and withdrew two of the few remaining twenty-dollar bills she had stolen from the ATM the day before and placed them in the plate. Mrs. Brown noticed it and whispered, "My goodness, child, that's mighty generous of you, but you sure don't have to put that much money in the plate."

Faith told Mrs. Brown she wanted to "because that preacher man just gave me something that I really needed to hear and I feel like it's going to be valuable advice that could help me for the rest of my life." Mrs. Brown didn't ask Faith what she was talking about, but just smiled and passed the plate on down the pew.

After the lengthy church service was over and they had returned to the Brown's home, Faith thanked Mrs. Brown for her hospitality and told her that she had to be on her way.

Mrs. Brown replied, "Why are you in such a hurry to leave here, child? Where are you gonna go? Now that you've begun it, I think you should stay with us for a few more days and get your heart and mind filled with the love of Jesus. How about staying here with us for a few more days and go to my Bible study class that meets every night with me a few times so you can get to really know more about our dear Lord, Jesus?"

Faith didn't know how to respond to Mrs. Brown's kind invitation at first, but decided that maybe she was right. She realized that she had only touched the smallest tip of the iceberg in her newfound spirituality, and decided she would attend the Bible study group with Mrs. Brown for a few days in order to become more familiar with what she was sensing about how her spirituality could have a positive effect on her future. Besides, she didn't have anywhere else to go.

During one of her afternoon Bible study sessions, Faith whispered to Mrs. Brown, "How do you know that Jesus really exists when you've never actually personally seen Him or heard Him talk?"

Mrs. Brown replied, "Have you ever seen the wind, child? No, you haven't, but you can feel it and you know it's there, don't you? Have you ever seen the cold? No, you haven't, but you also feel it and know it's there. Many great and more educated people than you and me have spent their entire lives in studying Jesus and confirmed that He's for real, so who are we to challenge their wisdom? No, I can't prove that Jesus exists any more than I can prove that he doesn't; but the more you allow yourself to believe in Him, the more real He becomes in your life."

Faith then asked her, "The preacher told us we should pray to God as often as we can. How can God hear millions of prayers at once and respond to all of them, Mrs. Brown? That seems impossible to me that a single person could do that."

"Well, child, have you ever heard of a computer? The big computers can handle millions of transactions at once, can't they? Since the Creator of all things enabled man to make a computer, don't you think God can handle messages better than something that we created? Child, when you think of our God, you gotta think big and not in small human terms because He created us and is powerful and loving beyond our wildest imagination."

Mrs. Brown always had a logical and satisfactory answer to every doubt that Faith raised!

After spending the rest of the week in going with Mrs. Brown to her nightly Bible study group, during which time her son, Jeremy, had made a few vain attempts to become personal with Faith and which she firmly rebuffed, she finally decided it was time to move on and be on her own again.

Faith said, "I've got to go away and do some real serious thinking about a lot of things, Mrs. Brown, and hope you'll understand why I must leave you for now and be by myself for awhile.

You've helped me more than I could ever tell you to better know and understand a lot of important things about myself and especially about our Jesus; and it's now time for me to carry it out into the world with me and restart my new life with Him to guide me."

Mrs. Brown didn't argue with Faith but gave her a hug, wished her well, told her she would pray for her every day, and that she was always welcome to come back any time she needed a place to stay.

Faith left Mrs. Brown's home and began walking aimlessly down the street by herself without a clue as to where she was headed, but she tightly held on to the envelope in her pocket with the moving words the pastor had said the week before written on it, and kept repeating the message to herself.

She thought as she walked. *I've got to start thinking beyond the moment instead of only where I will get the next candy bar, because I'd rather kill myself than keep on living the horrible and unhappy way I have all my life. There just has to be a better way for me to live. What do I want to be?*

She continued to ponder the question the pastor had instilled into her mind over and over...*what do I want to be? I really don't have a clue yet, but I'm sure as heck going to find out, whatever it takes.* Faith re-directed her thoughts when she saw a sign that read *Carolina Beach 10 miles.*

She thought, *I've heard lots of people talk about how beautiful and fun the beach was for them, and that's where I think I need to go to do some really serious thinking about what I want to do with my life. Maybe I can even sleep on the beach until something better comes along.*

Despite the wet and windy day and the blisters she

was getting on her feet from doing more walking than she had ever done in her entire life, Faith continued walking on towards Carolina Beach. Nearly four hours later, she found herself walking across the long Snow's Cut Bridge, which leads across the inlet and into Carolina Beach.

# Chapter Six

It was an early fall day and Faith found this place she had heard so many nice things about to be windy, rainy, and nearly deserted, with only a few cars on the street and a very small number of people outside.

As she walked alone in the light drizzling rain, she felt the urge to have another candy bar. Without thinking, she reached into her bag to retrieve one, and then suddenly stopped. As she stared at the candy bar in her hand, she thought to herself, *No! I won't do it...I hereby promise that I will never eat another damned candy bar for the rest of my life, so help me Jesus. Yes, my dear Jesus, please help me...I really do need Your help on that one!*

She quickly dumped out the package of candy bars from her bag and tossed them into a trash can. She then dropped to her knees, bowed her head, clasped her hands together and said, "Dear Jesus, if you are real, and I want to believe you are because you are the only hope I have left in this world, please help me to change my miserable and meaningless life into one that's happy and meaningful, and not like the horrible one I've lived ever since the day I was born."

Faith arose from her knees and felt uplifted and moving towards her new purpose. She was filled with confidence and excitement about the new life that she believed was soon forthcoming and was going to produce the real happiness that had eluded her until now.

This brief period of euphoric feeling which Faith was experiencing in her mind was suddenly interrupted by the voice of a policeman standing behind her who asked, "Young lady, are you alright?"

Fearing that the policeman might recognize and arrest her, Faith replied, "Yes I am alright, officer, and thank you for asking. I was just saying a prayer to Jesus, if that's okay."

The policeman replied, "That's fine, m'am, and I didn't mean to bother you; I just wanted to make sure you were okay, so you go right ahead and say your prayers and have yourself a nice day."

Relieved that the friendly officer hadn't recognized and arrested her, Faith continued to walk along towards the beach, a place that she had heard so many nice things about but had never actually seen. The ocean waves were high, the sky was beginning to clear up, and it was becoming a beautiful warm fall day on the beach!

When she reached the beach, she removed her shoes and socks and placed them in her bag, rolled her pants legs up to her calves, which was as far as her fat legs would allow, and began slowly walking along the water's edge with her hot and blistered feet being cooled off by the relaxing ocean water.

As Faith walked, she was in deep concentration as she pondered over what she should do with her future life, and the calming effects of the ocean waves seemed to relax and help her think more clearly than she ever had been able to before.

Between thoughts, Faith would say a prayer to Jesus and ask Him to provide her with the strength, wisdom, and courage to discover and follow the correct way to go that would bring her lofty new aspiration to be all she could be into reality. In her very deep state of thought, she had wandered out into the ocean a little further than she realized when a large wave suddenly struck and knocked her over into the water!

She stood up and struggled ashore; soaking wet, but still excited over her personal epiphany and had a happy smile on her face...the first real smile she could remember ever having, and it felt so good! Although she was only fourteen years old, Faith's interest in and confidence about her future was strong and it was the first time in her life that she had ever felt as good about anything.

As she stood on the beach shaking the water off of herself and the soaking wet bag of clothes, a thin and elderly lady who appeared to be at least in her eighties or better waved to Faith and ran gracefully past her like a deer.

Faith stood and watched the slender, grey-haired lady as she nearly disappeared about a mile down the beach; then, to Faith's surprise, she turned around and headed back towards the spot where Faith was standing.

As the lady approached, Faith waved to her and said, "Good day, m'am...you are an absolutely amazing woman!" The lady stopped and Faith asked, "If you don't mind my asking you, m'am, how in the world do you manage to stay in such good shape at your age?"

The older lady smiled and said, "And a good day to you, too, young lady. Please don't be offended by what I'm going to say, but I once weighed a lot more than you and I finally realized that I had to do something about it or continue leading the miserable life that my being overweight was causing me.

It took a good while for me to change my lifestyle, and it sure wasn't comfortable at the beginning, but I went from looking like a beached whale to what I am now. I just turned eighty-five years old and I feel and think I look better than I did when I was more than fifty years younger."

Faith thanked her for sharing her story and told her that she was trying to deal with the same problem and hoped she would someday be able to accomplish with her fat body what the old lady had with hers.

The woman replied, "You're quite welcome, young lady, and I wish you the very best in dealing with your challenge. I have the feeling that you're really serious about changing your life and will make it happen. By the way, let me introduce myself. My name is Ruth Dickson and I run along the beach around this time every day, and you're more than welcome to join me if you wish."

Faith said, "That's awfully sweet of you, Mrs. Dickson, but I don't think I could run more than a hundred yards, if that much; much less run the huge distance and as fast as you just did. My name is Faith."

Mrs. Dickson replied, "It's really not as hard as it may seem to you, Faith. You just start out by doing a little more each day and you'll be surprised at how soon you'll be running along like me all the way. And, Faith, please call me Ruth, because you make me feel like an old lady when you call me Mrs. Dickson," she said with a chuckle. "Do you live here at the beach, Faith?"

Faith answered, "No, m'am, I don't live here; I just got here but I'm planning on staying for a little while if I can find a place to stay that's not too expensive. Would you happen to know of one?"

Mrs. Dickson replied, "Everything here at Carolina Beach is pretty expensive, but you're welcome to stay over at my cottage with me tonight if you wish, Faith. My husband is going to be away on a trip for a few days and I sure could use some company because I'm not comfortable being alone. Besides, you've got to dry yourself and your belongings off, and you're very welcome to use my clothes dryer."

This was an answer to prayers for Faith! She needed somewhere to stay for the night and really liked the friendly feelings she was having with this kind old lady, so she gladly accepted her offer.

She followed Ruth to her "cottage" which, from Faith's perspective, turned out to be more like a *mansion* than a cottage. It had four bedrooms, four and a half bathrooms, a huge kitchen, a large wraparound porch, a two-car garage, and a very large open den with a stone fireplace. Faith had never been in or even imagined such a luxurious place existed in her entire fourteen years!

Ruth led Faith to an elegantly furnished bedroom that was more like a suite, and was a decorator's dream! It had a queen-sized bed, private bath, sitting area, and even its own large television set. Faith was overwhelmed with its magnificence!

Ruth said, "I think you've had yourself a pretty busy day because you look sort of tired, young lady, so why don't you come into the den and let's chat for a few minutes; then we'll have ourselves a little snack before we go to bed."

Faith thanked her and they went into the kitchen where Ruth removed a platter from the refrigerator that was filled with celery stuffed with cottage cheese, pieces of cold turkey, and apple slices, and offered the delicious snacks to Faith.

After they had finished their nighttime snack, they chatted for awhile and Ruth asked Faith, "Would you like to join me in my nightly prayer before you go to bed, Faith? My husband, John, and I usually say a prayer together after we finish our nighttime snack and before we go to bed."

"Yes, m'am, I mean Ruth...that would be nice except I

don't really know how to pray very well. Would you mind doing it for both of us?"

"Sure, sweetie, I'll start our prayer and you can enter in to it any time you want to. Just think of it as you and I having a friendly little chat with God and Jesus." Ruth began with the Lord's Prayer, which Faith vaguely recalled hearing Reverend Johnson saying at Ella Mae Brown's church and thought it sounded real nice, and then started her individual prayer.

"Dear heavenly Father, we deeply thank you for giving us our wonderful lives and for always guiding us in the right direction. We also thank you for this surprise meeting between Faith and me, one which I sense will prove to be a good thing for both of us as we get to know each other better.

Please help both of us to stay focused on the positive things in our lives and keep us ever mindful of the needs of those who are less fortunate than us." Then she asked, "Faith, would you care to add anything to our chat with God and Jesus?"

Faith didn't hesitate and said, "Thank you, God and Jesus, for bringing my new friend, Ruth, into my life and please keep me strong in my commitment to be all I can be for You."

Ruth added, "and for yourself as well, Faith." They then said "amen" together, stood, hugged, and went to their respective bedrooms for the evening. From the moment her head hit the soft pillow, Faith slept like a baby all night long in the most comfortable sleep she could recall ever having.

The following morning at six a.m., Ruth shook Faith and said, "Get yourself up and outta that bed, Miss Lazy Bones. I've dried and folded all your clothes, and laid them out on your settee. You and I have ourselves an important appointment to keep on the beach this morning, so get your running rags on and let's head outside for our first shape-up run together."

Faith really didn't want to leave the warm comfort of the bed and had feelings of anxiety about going for a run, knowing what bad shape she was in, but figured she'd better follow Ruth's instructions. So she crawled out of bed, put on a sweatshirt, shorts, and tennis shoes and met Ruth on the front porch as the sun was just beginning to rise over the beautiful Atlantic Ocean.

Ruth said, "Here's what we'll do honey. I know you're not quite ready to become a marathon runner yet, but if you stay with it, you'll get there sooner than you think. We'll start by walking together briskly for a little bit to loosen up until you begin to feel about ready; and then force yourself to do a little running with whatever energy you have until you have to stop, even if it's for just a few yards. Remember where you had to stop this morning and try to add a few yards to your stopping spot when we run again later on this afternoon. Okay?"

For the first time, Faith was more determined to succeed than she was fearful of failing, so they began walking at what was, for Faith, a pretty fast pace. After they had walked down the beach for about a hundred yards, she raised her hand and said through gasping breaths, "Ruth, I think I'm already beginning to run out of gas now."

Ruth said, "Okay, Faith, now take off in a run with all the energy you have left in you."

Faith ran for about fifty yards more and was ready to quit, but kept pushing herself for another twenty-five yards or so, and then collapsed on the beach, exhausted. Ruth waved goodbye and continued to run down the beach like a small race horse until she was out of sight. A few minutes later she returned and stopped where

Faith was still sitting on the sand, puffing hard to get her breath back.

Ruth said, "That was a mighty fine beginning for you, Faith. You can add a little more on to it when we go for another run again this afternoon."

Faith smilingly replied, "Well, like you said, Ruth, it was only a beginning. The next time, I'll do a little better and try to add a few more yards."

They returned to Ruth's home where they both showered, and then sat out on the deck of Ruth's home sipping green tea and eating a tasty fruit and vegetable salad that Ruth had prepared earlier.

As they sat together eating their salads, Ruth asked, "How about telling me a little bit about yourself, Faith... like how old you are, where you're from, what brings you to Carolina Beach, what you do for a living, and about your family? I hope you won't think I'm being too nosey to ask you these things but I like you and just want to get to know you better."

Faith hesitated for a few moments and then replied. "I was about to tell you a bunch of made up lies about myself, Ruth; not to impress you but to avoid your knowing the truth about me, because I fear that when you hear my story, which I'm going to tell you honestly for the first time in my life anyhow, you'll probably want me to immediately leave your beautiful home. If you should prefer that I leave then, I will understand and go.

I might as well begin with the worst thing. You probably think I'm a whole lot older than I am because of my large size, but I'm actually only fourteen years old. I was in my first year of high school and living in an orphanage in Fayetteville until a little over a week ago when I ran away. Both of my parents died several years ago and they were pathetic and unhappy people. I hardly remember them at all.

I've never had a happy moment in my life except the times when I was feeding my fat face, until some wonderful things happened to me during this past week. I've discovered God and Jesus, and I'm now the happiest girl I've ever been and I intend to stay that way, God willing. I'm sure you will probably want me to leave you after hearing my awful story, Ruth, which I will understand, so I'll thank you for your hospitality and just head on out to find me another place to stay if you want me to."

As she started to stand, Ruth pulled Faith close to her, hugged and kissed her on the cheek. "No, honey, you're not going anywhere...you're at *home*, and you are welcome to stay here with my husband and me for as long as you wish."

They both stood together, teary-eyed and hugging. Then Ruth said, "Well sit your sweet self down, my dear. Since you were good enough to honestly share your story with me, I'll do the same for you and tell you my own crazy story. Maybe it'll make *you* want to leave me!

You see, I was also once a very overweight girl for as long as I can remember until I was close to the age of thirty. Although I was blessed with a nice home and loving parents, they never put any pressure on me to stop gaining weight because they were also sort of on the chunky side themselves. I guess they felt they might hurt my feelings if they criticized me for my weight, which they really should have done, but they didn't...so up my weight steadily went nearly every day until I finally zoomed way past the two hundred pound mark.

I had no real friends or much of a social life of any sort and had never had a boy friend, other than an occasional boy who just wanted to use me for his pleasure.

I did manage to finish college at the University of North Carolina in Wilmington with a bachelor's degree in education and I then taught eighth grade English for a few years at a junior high school in Wilmington. But I was laid off during a supposed reduction in staff... and I was the *only* teacher in the entire system that it happened to. In looking back, there's no doubt in my mind but that the principal let me go because I was as large as I was and was on the cusp of developing adult onset diabetes.

I then looked everywhere for a job, but no one would hire me, not even the fast food joints or cleaning services. Although no one would dare say it to my face, I knew full well what the real reason was for them rejecting me; it was simply because I was too damned fat!

One day while I was in downtown Wilmington, haplessly looking for a job, I walked past the Army Recruiting Office. Acting on an impulse, I decided to stop in and find out what I could about possibly joining the Army since I had to find something to do with my life.

The recruiting sergeant was very polite and nice to me, but she told me there was absolutely no way I could get into the Army unless I could lose at least seventy pounds. I was broken hearted to hear yet another rejection and had unhappy tears streaming down my face.

The kindly sergeant put my hand in hers and told me that she felt sorry for me. She went on to tell me I could join a pre-enlistment physical fitness group that worked out every evening at a nearby high school gym if I wished, and would be able to join the Army if and when I could get myself within the Army's maximum allowable weight limits.

Like I'm sure you can well understand, Faith, I was angry and depressed as hell from being reminded for the thousandth time about how fat I was! I left the recruiting office in a huff and then went home and ate a large bag of potato chips and drank a six-pack of beer to drown my sorrows and quell my anger, and it made me sicker than a dog.

After being on my knees at the toilet from puking up the beer and potato chips, I took a deep breath and pleaded to God to please show me the way out of my miserable life and into a happy one. When I crawled into my bed that night, I stayed awake almost all night long with a picture in my mind of the banner that was hanging outside the Army recruiting office that read, "Be All You Can Be." Reflecting back, I believe seeing that sign was the biggest turning moment in my life!

After going through over five months of tortuous physical training and nearly starving myself down seventy pounds I was finally able to enlist in the Army as a Private. I was trained at Fort Sam Houston, Texas to be a combat medic, something completely unrelated to my past, but I enjoyed it. Then, while I was later serving in the Army at the Womack Army Hospital at Fort Bragg, I met John, the man whom I would later marry.

John was also a soldier who was from the nearby town of Leland. He was a sergeant in the Army's Special Forces and later went to fight in Viet Nam. He returned home minus a leg that he lost while in the jungle on a combat operation, and was later medically discharged. After we had both finished our military service as sergeants, we came back to Wilmington and were married.

John had always been a very spiritually minded fellow and wanted to become a minister; so he entered into a seminary in Virginia, from which he later graduated, and was ordained as an Episcopal priest.

After graduating from the seminary, John became the pastor of a small church outside of Wilmington for his first three years, and then took charge as the rector of a very large one in Wilmington where he served for over forty years. I earned my Master's degree in counseling at UNC-Wilmington and then worked as a high school counselor for several years until we both retired.

When I was almost forty, we had a late in life daughter, Christina, who was absolutely beautiful beyond words. Unlike I had been earlier in my life; she was very fit, athletic, attractive, and sociable. When she would come home on weekends, Christina and I used to love to go running together on the beach like you and I are now doing.

Christina was the class valedictorian in her high school, sang in the school chorus, played on her school's girls basketball team, taught a Sunday school class in my husband's church, and was only a week away from graduating summa cum laude with a degree in education from the Methodist University in Fayetteville, and had made plans to continue on and pursue her master's degree.

Then, on a weekend drive home just one week before her graduation from the university, her car was struck by a drunk driver near Elizabethtown and she was instantly killed. I don't think I'll ever be able to get over losing her because I miss her all the time, but I'm happy in knowing that she's in a better place with our Lord." The entire time Ruth was talking, a steady stream of tears was pouring down her cheeks.

When Ruth finished, Faith held her close and said, "Thank you for sharing your very touching story with me, Ruth. You're such a beautiful and wonderful lady and I'm really so honored to know you. And I can't believe that we both share the same motto as our guiding philosophy, to be all we can be. That is so amazing!"

Ruth wiped away her tears and said, "Thanks, Faith, and you are one beautiful young lady inside...and you're gonna soon be just as beautiful on the outside, because you and I are gonna run some of those pounds off of you, my soon-to-be regular little running buddy. You're gonna be all you can be, I promise, or I'll kick your sweet butt!"

Ruth and Faith began running together twice every day, and Faith would add a little more distance each time.

Five days later, Ruth's husband, John, returned home from his trip, where had had been a guest lecturer at his old seminary and attended his class reunion. He was a handsome, grey-haired, and physically fit gentleman who sounded almost like Johnny Cash when he spoke with his deep baritone voice. He walked without a limp even though he wore a prosthetic device from where he had lost one of his legs just below the knee from when he stepped on a land mine during the Viet Nam war.

Ruth introduced Faith to John who gave her a warm welcoming hug and said, "I'm so glad to meet you, Faith, and thank you so much for taking care of my precious wife while I was away because I feel uncomfortable when she's here alone. I'm afraid she might find herself a younger boy friend with two real legs and leave me," he said with a laugh. "She told me some mighty nice things about you on the telephone, Faith; most of all that she has a new running buddy."

Faith replied, "It's been so nice for me to be friends with your lovely wife as well, Reverend, and I'm so honored to meet you after she told me so many nice things about you. I hope I haven't been too much of a bother to you all, but I'll plan on leaving early in the morning so you two wonderful people can have yourselves a little time alone together."

Ruth piped in, "Oh no; you're not going anywhere, young lady! You're my new running partner and I need to have you here to run with me. I love my dear husband with all my heart, but he just doesn't understand girly talk the way we do, and he always runs a lot faster than I do…even with his funny-looking, fake, man-made leg."

John laughed and said, "Hey, now please take it easy, girls. It's been a long day for all of us, so let's all hit the sack now and we can talk about this stuff in the morning, okay?" They all then went to bed. To her pleasant surprise, Faith was pretty certain that she could hear John and Ruth happily making love in their bedroom during the night!

Although Faith was so happy in her current environment with the Dickson's, she was beginning to feel some anxiety over what her next move should be and was experiencing some difficulty in getting to sleep that night.

She would have occasional thoughts of being apprehended by the law and taken back to Fayetteville to face prosecution for her crimes. The thought of having to leave this wonderful place where she was feeling the happiest she had in her entire life and probably being sent to prison for her several offenses was becoming an increasing source of anxiety to her.

Early the next morning, Ruth awakened Faith. "Okay, my dear young running buddy, get your lazy and soon to be little butt outta that sack and let's head out for the beach and go for our first run of the day."

John, Ruth, and Faith dressed and went outside. It was a beautiful fall day with a slightly tepid breeze blowing in from the ocean. John waved to Faith and Ruth and laughingly said, "I'll see you two slowpoke gals later; and then took off running down the beach like a rabbit with his metal prosthetic leg making a strange scraping noise and kicking up the sand.

Ruth asked Faith, "Are you ready to take off on our run, my little running buddy?"

Faith laughingly replied, "Yep, I'm about as ready as

I'm gonna be, and I am proud to be your running buddy; but I'm sure as heck not little...not yet, anyhow, but I'm darned well gonna get there with the help you've given me to get started, Ruth. Let's get a-going!"

After they had walked together for a couple of hundred yards to warm up, Ruth took off in a run with Faith running alongside of her. Faith ran for all she was worth, passing her last stopping point from the day before and going at her top speed for almost another two hundred yards, and finally stopped...exhausted and out of breath, but with a wide grin on her face. "I can't believe I can already run this fast and this far, Ruth!"

"I can believe it, my child, and you did it, by golly." She hugged Faith and said, "I'm so proud of you, Sweetie!"

Faith tearfully hugged her back and said, "You did it for me...you and God. I love you both so much, Ruth."

"And we love you, too," Ruth replied and then took off to complete her run.

When they returned to the Dickson's home, Ruth presented Faith with a package that was nicely wrapped and had a pretty red bow on top. "This is gonna be one of your friends for the future, my little running buddy."

Faith opened the package and it contained an expensive-looking scale with an engraved plaque on it that read, *I Will Be All That I Can Be.*

Ruth said, "This scale used to be mine and I used it every day. Now it's yours to measure your daily success. Now go put your present in your bathroom right now, because you're not gonna go anywhere anytime soon, young lady."

# Chapter Seven

Several days later, after completing their usual morning run, to which Faith had already added nearly a half-mile, John, Ruth, and Faith sat together on the Dickson's oceanfront deck while they enjoyed a healthy breakfast of fresh fruit and green tea.

With a serious look on his face, John said to Faith in his deep baritone voice, "Honey, there are some things that we need to take care of in order to help protect you. From what Ruth has shared with me, you're a minor who's on the lam and are probably being looked for by the law as we speak. I hope you know that we both love and want to help you, and there are certain things we need to do in order to help get you out of your legal situation and protect ourselves from trouble as well.

I'm going to get in touch with an attorney friend of mine in Raleigh later today and seek his guidance on what he thinks needs to be done in order to help you clear up this mess in your life, and we'll do whatever he recommends to us. Are you okay with that, Faith?"

In her happy new life with the Dickson's, Faith didn't completely understand what she should do, nor had she given enough clear thought about what kind of consequences she must eventually have to face from her old life as a runaway, especially for committing the crimes of larceny from Mary Kay and the criminal assault on Wally...but she had confidence that the Dickson's would help her find the right way to deal with this challenge.

She meekly answered, "Yes, sir, I sure do appreciate your offer to help me, and promise I'll do whatever you say for me to do."

Ruth hugged her and said, "No matter what has to be done to help get you out of this mess, honey, we want you to know that we'll be standing beside you all the way until we get all of this legal crap cleared up and behind you so you can continue to grow in your wonderful newfound life."

Faith began to weep and said in a choking voice, "I never want to do anything that might bring trouble to you, my beautiful best friends. If I have to go back to Fayetteville, or even go to jail for awhile, I'll do it, but I have to admit that the very thought of it nearly scares me to death. Most of all, I don't want to risk losing the friendship of you two wonderful people. I don't want you to be upset by my saying this, but I sort of view you two dear folks as the parents I wish I had been born with."

Ruth replied, "You don't upset us by saying that, Faith; you *honor* us by being here with us, and we view you as a gift sent to us from God to help us ease the pain that we've never stopped feeling since the terrible day when we lost our dear Christina."

The three of them stood and hugged together, and then John said, "Okay, girls, since the ocean's looking so calm today let's stop all this tear-jerking girly talk and go for a nice swim. The last one in the water is a rotten egg!"

\*\*\*

Meanwhile, back in Fayetteville, all hell had been

breaking loose over Faith's disappearance! The State Police, Cumberland County Sheriff's Department, Fayetteville Police, and Army National Guard were all involved in a massive search for Faith, and large groups of volunteers and police dogs combed nearly every square inch between the orphanage and the trailer park in Tar Heel searching for her with no success.

Over a month had passed since Faith was first reported as missing and had been charged with several criminal offenses, and her story was printed each day in the daily newspaper, *The Fayetteville Observer,* and given heavy coverage by all of the area television stations.

One of the newspaper's mainstay columnists, Bill Kirby, whose warm wisdom and unique folksy style of writing had been read and appreciated by his reading fans in the County for many years, had researched Faith's past and wrote a touching and sympathetic story about her plight.

Kirby's column closed with, "Let us pray that this poor child has either found herself a better life somewhere on this earth, or is in an even better place with our Lord." His touching column received many complimentary letters to the editor, most expressing a deep and caring sympathy for Faith by the majority of his readers, and a small few who expressed their outright anger towards Faith for the bad things she had done.

\*\*\*

When they returned home from their enjoyable swim, where they had laughed, splashed water in each other's face, picked up several pretty sea shells, and had a jolly good time, John had a voice mail message from Alan Schneider, a well-known and distinguished Raleigh attorney whom John had known from many years ago.

Alan had defended John from a frivolous law suit that had been filed against him by a crazy, hippie-type, anti-war protesting lawyer back in the early seventies for having "killed innocent Vietnamese children," which wasn't true.

The suit was quickly dismissed by the presiding judge based on Alan's brilliant handling of the case, and also resulted in the hippie lawyer being severely sanctioned by the State Bar Association. John returned Alan's call from his office with the speakerphone turned on.

Alan answered and said, "John, my old friend, I had my staff do a lot of research on the background of the child you requested that we check out, and it really doesn't look very good.

It seems that the young girl has been in and out of an awful lot of trouble for the majority of her life, mostly over petty stuff. She has a pretty crappy school record, stole some money and other things from a woman at the orphanage that she lived in, and has three outstanding warrants for her arrest for larceny from a bank, theft of property, and an assault and battery on another lawbreaker. I also saw a photograph of her from her file at the orphanage, and she's quite a large sized gal for her age."

John replied, "I know she's done some pretty awful things, Alan, and she has already admitted all of these things to Ruth and me. We would like to get her cleared of these charges against her if that's at all possible, and we might even consider adopting her later on after this mess is over if it can be done. I agree with you that she's a very troubled child, but I don't believe she's really the evil person that some of the media have depicted her as being. What do you think we should do?"

Alan replied, "Let me do a little more checking around and talk with a friend of mine who's the District Attorney in Fayetteville and has the warrants out against her, and I'll get back to you on that in a day or so.

Are you and Ruth really serious about wanting to adopt her, John? After all, you told me she's only been with you all for a couple of weeks. Based on what she's accused of doing to a fellow in Tar Heel, whom she apparently tried to kill, she could be dangerous, pal; so you and Ruth please be very careful."

John said, "I really appreciate your advice, Alan, and your willingness to help us out, but I don't think she'd do anything to harm us. To be honest, I'm about seventy-five percent and growing in favor of wanting to adopt Faith and Ruth is already a hundred percent plus on the adoption matter and wants to help her real bad, whatever it takes, and so do I."

Alan replied, "That's awfully nice of you and Ruth to care for her, John, but there's another thing you must be aware of about this issue. You both could be charged with harboring as well as aiding and abetting a potential convicted felon, and those are serious criminal offenses that could even land you and Ruth in hot water, and maybe even some time in jail if the authorities should want to go after you, and I'd sure hate to see something that awful to happen to you two good friends."

John said, "Okay, Alan, I understand what you're saying and we deeply appreciate your concerns for us. We do understand the risks that we could face by helping her; but we feel that she's absolutely worth our taking the chance for. As you correctly say, we'll just have to be careful.

It'll take me a couple of days to get to the bottom of all this with her from this end, and we'll talk with you again as soon as you speak with the Cumberland County District Attorney and we know for sure what is best for us to do. Thanks a ton for your caring and for your always valued friendship, Alan."

Unbeknownst to John, Faith was standing in the hallway outside of his office and heard the entire conversation he had with his attorney friend. This deeply upset her, and she then quickly left the Dickson's home and went for a long walk on the beach by herself. She viewed this as yet another joyful experience in her life that was about to turn into a huge disappointment. She pondered over her options as she walked.

She thought to herself, *I've already grown to love these wonderful people so much, and I just can't allow them to get themselves into a lot of trouble because of the stupid things that I've done...but I just don't want to leave them. I don't have anywhere else to turn to and just don't know what I should do. Maybe I should just turn myself in right now and face the music for my stupidity and let them put me in jail. I want to be all that I can be, but being an inmate in a prison is definitely not one of those things that I want to be. Oh, dear God, please help me to know and do the right thing!*

In her confused and anxious mental state, Faith wandered around the beach area for awhile pondering the situation, and she soon found herself standing at the counter of a beachfront convenience store where, without thinking, she had purchased a king-sized Baby Ruth candy bar.

When she walked out of the store and removed the candy bar from her bag, Faith stopped and began to cry when she realized what she was about to do. She then quickly ran to the ocean's edge and threw the unopened candy bar out into the water as far as she could, and then ran back to the Dickson's home.

When she returned back to the house, Ruth rushed up to her and gave her a big hug. "Where in the world have you been, honey? We've been worried to death and have been looking all over the area for you."

Faith sadly replied, "I had to be by myself for a while and do some real serious thinking about my situation, Ruth. I know I've put you and your wonderful husband in a difficult position by your allowing me to be here in your home after all of the bad things I've done.

I promised you that I'll not lie to you now or ever, but I accidentally overheard Reverend Dickson talking to his lawyer on the phone a little while ago and heard the lawyer tell him that I could get you all into a lot of trouble and you could even have to go to jail for taking care of me, and it really upsets more than you know. As much as my being with you wonderful people has meant to me, because it's truly been the very best time of my whole life, I feel like I should go ahead and turn myself in now and face the consequences of my stupidity and leave you all, even if it means that I'll have to go to jail for awhile."

John walked into the room as they were talking and said, "I wasn't eavesdropping, either, but I heard what you just said to Ruth, Faith. I salute you for your courage in being willing to face the music with the law in order to avoid any trouble for us, but I don't think we're ready to do anything just yet...at least not until I hear back from Alan, my attorney friend in Raleigh. Then we'll put our heads together and come up with a game plan to help you out of this mess."

Ruth added, "Honey, you can be sure that we're going to stand beside you throughout this mess until it's over and you will be able to continue on in your new discovery of yourself, so let's not do anything just yet. In fact, let's you and I go for our daily beach run right now and get some of these worries off our minds for awhile, okay?"

As they walked together on the beach, Ruth told Faith how impressed she was with her rapidly growing maturity, high moral standards, and courage, and how she viewed her as being intelligent and wonderful like their daughter, Christina, had been before they lost her.

With tears rolling down her cheeks, Faith hugged her and said, "I love you so much, Ruth. Would it bother you if I call you *Mom,* instead of Ruth, because that's what you're like to me...the mom that I always wanted but never had until just a couple of weeks ago when you came into my life."

Ruth was choked with tears and said, "Okay, my new *daughter,* I'm honored to be called your mom; now stop your stalling and let's knock off all this tear-jerking stuff and get on with our run."

They began their run together and Faith blew past her previous stopping points like an antelope, and kept going until she had run for nearly a mile! She finally ran out of breath, came to a stop, fell to her knees, and exhaustedly said, "I'm not there with your distance yet, Mom, but I promise you that I'm gonna keep working on it and get there real soon!"

When they returned to the house, Faith went to her room and stepped on the scales Ruth had given her three days before and saw she had already lost a little more than five pounds in the past three days. She was elated and said to herself as she stared into the mirror, "Faith, my girl, you ain't seen nothing yet because I promise that you're gonna be a darned good-looking chick one of these days real soon!"

Faith happily reported her weight loss to Ruth who said, "Let's all go out together and celebrate your new success with a nice dinner tonight. We'll go to a restaurant we like that's close by and where they serve fantastic light, diet-oriented, broiled seafood dinners. Would you like to do that?"

Faith replied, "That'd sure be a wonderful new treat

for me, Mom, because I've never been out to dinner in a real restaurant in my entire life."

Ruth, John, and Faith walked to the restaurant together. After they were inside and seated, Faith excused herself and went to the ladies room to wash her hands. As she walked past the front of the restaurant, the cashier stared real hard at Faith and asked, "Excuse me, Miss; don't I know you from somewhere? You sure do look real familiar to me."

Faith replied, "No, m'am; I don't think we've met since I've never been here before."

"I just feel as though I've seen you somewhere before", said the cashier. Then it suddenly popped into her mind that she had seen Faith's picture on the television news and in newspaper stories about her being a sought-after criminal fugitive, so she immediately telephoned her boyfriend who was a local police officer.

A few minutes later, as the threesome were enjoying their dinner, two police officers entered the restaurant and the cashier pointed them to the Dickson's table.

One of the officers walked to the table and politely asked, "Excuse me Miss, would your name be Faith Thomas?"

Faith smilingly replied, "Yes sir, it is."

He then grimly said, "We have a warrant for your arrest, Miss Thomas. Now please stand up and turn around so we may place handcuffs on you."

With Ruth sobbing and John holding her, the officers took the handcuffed and teary-eyed Faith outside, placed her into the back seat of a police car, and drove off to the Carolina Beach jail.

Faith was strip searched by a lady police officer and given an orange jail jumpsuit to wear, then locked in a cell at the Carolina Beach Police Station. The police supervisor on duty advised her as to why she was being detained and told her the Cumberland County Sheriff's Department would be sending a car over to pick her up early the next morning to take her back to Fayetteville and face the charges against her.

That night, as she struggled to sleep on the hard jail cot, unhappy thoughts of what lay ahead ran through Faith's head. Just the day before, she had been the happiest she had ever been in her entire life while living with Ruth and John; and now she was facing possible incarceration, and for how long it might be she had no idea. She had heard many horror stories about how awful it would be for her to be in prison and these thoughts frightened her beyond words.

Finally, sometime in the wee hours of the morning, she knelt beside her bunk and said a prayer. "Dear God, I know I have no right to ask it, because I know I've been a bad girl for all of my life, but please give me the strength to deal with what I'm now facing without losing my commitment to be all I can be. Bless the wonderful Dickson family that loves me and I love with all my heart, and please someday allow us to be together again. I want to be a good girl, so please help me be that. Amen."

After Faith had said her prayer, her anxiety level went down a little, although she still knew that what she had to face was not going to be easy. She was awakened early the next morning by the same jailer who had locked her up the night before and told that a Cumberland County Sheriff's Department deputy had arrived to take her back to Fayetteville.

The female Cumberland County deputy sheriff handcuffed Faith and led her to a patrol car, then had her sit in the back seat with the door and window locks set. As they rode up Highway 87 North towards Fayetteville, the deputy tried to engage Faith in friendly conversation, but she was pretty quiet and unresponsive because her troubled mind was elsewhere. After a quiet hour and a half drive, they arrived in Fayetteville where Faith was processed in to the Cumberland County Detention Center.

# Chapter Eight

O n the following day, Faith made her first court appearance, which was done via closed-circuit television from the County Detention Center to the courtroom where the charges were read to her and she was assigned a public defender attorney.

Although she was still feeling some surges of anger and even an occasional bit of craving for sweets when things didn't seem to be going her way, Faith stayed strong with her commitment to not give in to them, and was polite and compliant with the directions of the Detention Center's staff. Because of the nature of her offenses, Faith was being treated as an adult.

As she sat in her cell, Faith was still deep in thought over trying to decide what she wanted to be after whatever she had to face was over, remaining steadfast in her determined commitment to herself in striving to be all she could be, regardless of what she had to face, and keeping in mind that the frightful challenges that were confronting her would eventually pass behind her.

Later that morning, a corrections officer told her that she had a visitor. She couldn't imagine who that could be. She thought to herself, *who besides the Dickson's could know that I'm here?*

The corrections officer handcuffed her and led her to

a small conference room where she was surprised to see her high school counselor, Cheryl Peters, waiting to see her!

Cheryl stood and put her arms around Faith. "I'm so glad to see that you're okay Faith. You sure are looking great, girl. Are they treating you right?"

Faith said, "Yes Ms. Peters, they've been more than kind to me; a whole lot kinder to me than I deserve to be treated after doing all the awful things I've done, and I can't tell you just how glad I am to see you again. You were always so good to me in spite of my immature behavior."

Cheryl replied, "I still care about you, Faith, and want you to know that I'm here to help you in any way I can. I just met your friends, the Dickson's, who are out in the jail lobby and are also here waiting to see you. They're the nicest folks and they seem to think the world of you. They allowed me to see you first since I've got to get back to work at the school pretty soon."

Faith said, "Yes, Ms. Peters, they are really dear friends of mine. They, you, and a Mrs. Ella Mae Brown in Wilmington have been so good to me and helped me to see things so differently, and caused me to finally want to turn my life around and live the right way. I'm really surprised that you didn't give up on me after all the trouble and embarrassment that I probably put you and the others through while I was at your school."

Cheryl replied, "I still believe in you, Faith, and I got the distinct impression from chatting with Reverend and Mrs. Dickson that you're finally beginning to believe in yourself as well. It really makes me feel so glad to hear that."

Faith smilingly replied, "Yes, m'am, the last few weeks have been a huge turning point in my life, Ms. Peters, and I finally have gotten some hope for myself and my future."

Cheryl said, "I spoke with the assistant district attorney, who's a friend of mine and will be prosecuting your case in court, Faith, and I got the impression from her that there's some sympathy for you from the District Attorney.

In fact, even the guy from Tar Heel who you were staying with, named Wallace Cochran, that you have been accused of assaulting, testified at his hearing yesterday that what happened to him really wasn't your fault...that he had given you just cause for doing what you did to him. Based on that, I understand that there's a fair chance that they may drop the assault and battery charge against you."

Faith replied, "That's very decent of him to admit that and, although he did some pretty awful things to me and hurt my feelings, I don't hold any ill feelings toward him. In fact, when I reflect back on it, I realize that most of the bad things I have experienced in my life, including what happened between Wally and me, were largely my own fault.

But what's more important to me now, Ms. Peters, is that this unhappy experience started a chain of happy new experiences that have lifted me up and given me a whole new outlook on my life and a better way to live it."

"Wow, young lady...and that's what you've become, Faith, a really fine young lady! I'm so impressed with how much you've matured in such a short period of time and how much better you look. It makes me feel good about my believing all along that you have some good stuff inside you, Faith, and you really do."

After a few more minutes of chatting, Cheryl rose and said, "Well, I've got to leave you for now, Faith, so the Dickson's can have some time to visit with you and I can get back to work, but you and I will definitely get together again soon."

Cheryl and Faith hugged; then, as Cheryl left the Dickson's were led in to the visiting room.

Ruth and Faith tearfully hugged each other so hard that it nearly took both of their breaths away!

They sat down at the table and John filled Faith in on the situation just as it had been explained to him by his friend, the Raleigh attorney. "Mr. Schneider spoke with the District Attorney and it seems that they're not at all happy about having to prosecute you, honey, and Ms. Peters told us that she heard from a friend that the thing with the boy in Tar Heel looks like it's going to be dropped.

Unfortunately, the theft of the girl's purse at the orphanage and the money taken from the bank will require that some punitive action be taken against you, and Alan believes it'll probably only be some supervised probation with no prison time. That's the good news."

Faith replied, "That's great to hear, Dad, and I can handle the probation or whatever else they decide for me to do. Is there some bad news?"

John said, "I'm afraid so, Faith. Alan thinks you'll probably be sent to either the State School for Unmanageable Children in Raleigh or maybe, with a little luck, you will be allowed to go back to the orphanage in Fayetteville where you lived before, to stay until you're either sixteen or have an acceptable home in which to live. I remember you telling us how you didn't like the orphanage and dreaded going to the State school even more, so I hope that doesn't have to be."

Ruth injected, "It sure wouldn't hurt for us to ask the judge if your being adopted and living with us would be possible so that you wouldn't have to go there. We have already retained a family attorney in Greensboro by the name of Carolyn Woodruff, who's a friend of Alan's, and she is going to help us to get the adoption process started. If the judge will allow it, and she seems to think it stands a good chance but will probably take as much as a year after your probation is over before it can actually happen, you could officially become our daughter."

"Oh my great God, that would be so wonderful, Mom! Are you sure you want an ugly fat girl with a criminal rap sheet like mine being your daughter and living with you and Dad in your beautiful home?" asked Faith.

Ruth replied, "Sweetie, you're not ugly and never have been; and you're not going to be fat in just a few more months because you've already lost a lot of weight and are beginning to look really great. And your rap sheet will be sealed when you reach age eighteen so all of that bad stuff will be behind you and won't interfere with your future life.

More than you'll ever know, we want you to become our daughter, providing that you'll continue to be my beach running partner. Will you be able to handle that?"

Faith's eyes swelled with tears as she looked up and said, "Yes! Yes! Yes! Thank you dear God for giving me the two most wonderful people on this planet as parents." Then all three hugged together and danced around in circles as they shared happy tears and laughter.

The happy meeting ended when a corrections officer opened the door and said, "Your visiting time is up so you folks will have to leave right now and I'll have to take you back to your cell, young lady."

Faith returned to her cell filled with a renewed confidence and great hope for the future, something that had never been a part of her earlier life.

Her cellmate was a young black woman named Clarice Shaw, who was facing charges for a drug possession and a driving while impaired offense, and she was also obese and very angry.

In what was a strange new role for her, Faith befriended the woman whose negative and hostile attitude towards life was quite similar to what Faith's had been. Faith understood what Clarice was feeling inside and was able to quickly enter into a friendly relationship with her, and soon even had her doing exercises and praying along with her. Faith got a good feeling in her heart from helping Clarice.

This discovery was yet another epiphany type experience for Faith...having a special insight into the misery of another person's obesity and helping her in finding ways to deal with it. The seed for a future *raison d'être* for herself, that of helping others who suffer from the same misery of obesity which she had, had been planted into Faith's mind!

Although she was unable to do any running while she was in jail, Faith did frequent sit-up and pushup exercises in her cell to maintain continuity in her battle with her weight, and encouraged Clarice to join her. She was also selective in her food, choosing only the healthiest foods in the jail dining facility and giving her desserts and other fattening foods to the really emaciated women who did need them.

Although not there yet, Faith had the good feeling of knowing that many of the burdens in her life, including her weight and legal issues, were going to soon be behind her...and that her life would become far better!

Her court-appointed defense attorney, Brandon Fortner, a newly licensed attorney and a medically retired former Special Forces Sergeant who had recently graduated from law school at UNC-Charlotte, met with Faith and provided her with an overview of what was ahead for her in her trial.

"Miss Thomas, while I sense that neither the prosecutor nor the judge in this case would want to hurt you beyond what you've already experienced, we can't depend entirely on their sympathy.

I want us to go into the courtroom fully prepared for anything that might come up, because you never know what else the prosecutor might try to throw at you. You and I have a special attorney/client privilege in that you may feel free in sharing anything you wish with me without having any fear of its coming back to haunt you later. How do you feel about your present situation?"

Faith replied, "Mr. Fortner, I know I've done a lot of wrong things in my young life that I shouldn't have done and were the result of my foolish anger, lack of spirituality, low sense of self-esteem, and a terribly fat body.

Perhaps one of the worst things I've done and something that I've already punished myself for so many times is my irresponsible negligence of my God-given body and that has affected my mind and entire life negatively. Beyond that, it's a fact that I did steal Miss Adams' purse and stole money from the bank, and feel I should be held accountable and punished for the wrong things I've done."

Brandon said, "I salute you for your mature and responsible thinking, Faith, but let's not stick your neck in the noose unnecessarily by asking for punishment. You're a young girl and now a clearly honest one who has suffered a lot in your young life, and that's what I want the judge to understand. If I am able to persuade the prosecutor to agree to it in return for a plea of guilty, how would you feel about accepting a year of supervised probation?"

"What does it mean to be on supervised probation, Mr. Fortner?"

"Basically, Faith, it means that you'll be accountable to the court for your nearly every action, including complete abstinence from any mind-altering substances such as alcohol or marijuana, a nightly curfew where you must be in your place of residence by a certain hour, attending school until you're at least sixteen years old, obeying all rules and laws, and whatever other conditions the judge may want to stipulate."

Faith replied, "That sounds more than fair, Mr. Fortner, and I'll gladly accept that and feel very blessed by it, because I certainly do deserve a lot more punishment than that for the awful things I've done."

Attorney Fortner gave her a reassuring hug and left; and Faith then returned to her cell with uplifted spirits. Despite her present good feelings, Faith knew deep inside that she was still on a very rocky road in her life and had many more steep hills to climb before she could become nearly satisfied with herself.

High among the important hills she would climb was in continuing in the growth of her relationship with God and keeping her relationship strong with Ella Mae Brown, Cheryl Peters, and Ruth and John together while she strived to become all she was capable of being.

At her trial, everything went pretty much as expected. Attorney Fortner was able to work out a good deal with the prosecutor and the judge sentenced her to one year of supervised probation. Two of the conditions that caused her some anxiety were that she must return to the orphanage she had left and remain there for the rest of the year, and must also return to her old high school.

Faith knew that her returning to these two past places of her earlier troubles would probably be an embarrassing challenge for her, but with her newfound courage she was prepared to accept the difficulties and embarrassment that her return to the orphanage and high school would probably bring.

High on her wish list was that the Dickson's would someday be allowed to have her live with them again at Carolina Beach as their daughter, but the judge required that she remain in Cumberland County for at least six more months with a clean record before he would allow her to even be considered for adoption or relocation.

When she was released from jail, Clarice gave Faith a warm goodbye hug and expressed her thanks to Faith for helping her to begin a new approach in living her life in a healthier, drug and alcohol free, and more moral way.

After an interview with her probation officer, who outlined the terms, conditions, and procedures related to her probation, Faith was allowed to leave the detention center. When she walked into the lobby, John and Ruth were standing there waiting for her. She rushed up to them and they shared happy hugs.

John said, "Honey, we're so glad this terrible situation is about to come to an acceptable ending. While the judge wouldn't permit the adoption to even be considered for at least six months, as far as we're concerned it's already happened in our hearts. We'll come and visit with you at the orphanage as often as we can, and can't wait until we can do what we all want, to permanently have you in our home at the beach as our daughter."

Ruth added, "Like John has told you, you are already our daughter in our hearts, and you'll be with us in your new home one day soon, honey. Your room will be waiting for you, and I'll be waiting for us to run together again when you're back at home with us."

Ironically, Mary Kay was sent by the orphanage director to pick Faith up from the detention center and drive her back to the orphanage. Mary Kay had especially requested to do this in order to give her an opportunity to express her forgiveness to Faith for what she had done to her.

Faith expressed her sincere apologies to Mary Kay and assured her that she would somehow find a way to repay her for the money she had stolen from her. Mary Kay accepted her apologies, hugged her, and assured her that she would help her in any way she could.

When they arrived back at the orphanage, Faith was brought to happy tears when she saw a banner made of a bed sheet and markers hanging in front of the orphanage's main building which said *Welcome home, Faith...we love you!* Ms. Sasser, the staff, and several of the children were standing in front of the building to welcome her.

After the pleasant welcoming event that was filled with warm hugs was over, Faith went to her old room and was pleased to find it had been decorated with a new bedspread, curtains, and fresh towels. Life was really beginning to look up!

On the following day, Faith boarded the orphanage bus for the trip to her high school. Although she was a little anxious about how she might be received by her classmates, she was determined to show them the "new" Faith.

When she entered her homeroom, her teacher, Miss Ploeger, was concerned as to how Faith would behave because of her former ugly outburst just a little over a month ago. Her concern quickly dissipated when Faith politely asked if she might be allowed to address her classmates, to which Miss Ploeger reluctantly consented.

With a tear trickling down her smiling cheek, Faith stood up before the class, cleared her throat and said, "My fellow classmates, I appreciate the opportunity to speak to you. I seek your forgiveness of me for the poor manner in which I behaved prior to my running away from my old life, and I hope you will allow me to be your classmate again in my newfound life. I promise to try and be a much better one than I was.

During the past few days, I have experienced some wonderful events which have enlightened me into realizing how wrong I have been in my past behavior, and how blessed I am to be back in school and be your classmate again. Thank you for allowing me to express myself."

The students stood and applauded Faith, and several walked up to her and gave her a warm and happy hug. Another hurdle had passed!

# Chapter Nine

The days that followed for Faith were definitely a one hundred and eighty degree turnabout in virtually every area from her previous immature, anger-driven, and irresponsible life.

She studied diligently, and brought her initially poor and failing grades up to all "A's," asked to return to the regular girl's physical fitness group where she not only kept up with the class in their runs but often came in first, and began building good friendly relationships with her peers.

She also tried out for and made the girls basketball team where she became a star point guard, and joined the school chorus where she sang a solo in the Christmas concert. Throughout this time, she continued to lose weight at the rate of about a pound a day, and was beginning to look like a new person...and a very attractive one at that!

Although she was looking good and had been asked to go on dates by several nice boys, Faith's scars from her traumatic experience with Wally hadn't healed and caused her to shy away from such activities.

She continued to work on her spiritual connection by regularly attending Sunday school and church at the nearby First Christian Church where she also sang in the choir, served as an acolyte, and helped out in the church nursery.

When the school year came to an end, Faith had made "A" pluses in all of her subjects and earned a place on the school's Honor Roll. Cheryl Peters nominated Faith as the school's *Most Outstanding Freshman Student of the Year,* which was unanimously approved by the Faculty Awards Committee. In her acceptance of this special award, Faith made a touching speech before the gathered student body.

"Members of the administration, faculty, and my fellow students, I am so highly honored to receive this award, but I certainly can't take full credit for it because there are others who helped me whom I would like to recognize. Each of these wonderful people have helped make it possible by their love, caring, guidance, and inspiration for me to change from being satisfied with what I was to wanting to be all I can be.

They include Ms. Cheryl Peters, whom you all know as a kind and dedicated professional counselor here in our school; a Mrs. Ella Mae Brown who lives in Wilmington, whom you probably wouldn't know; but it was she who introduced me to the person who led me from where I was and I know will continue to lead me in life, Jesus Christ, and my wonderful friends from Carolina Beach, Reverend and Mrs. John Dickson, whom I hope to one day have as my official parents. Thank all of you for helping me and giving me such a nice honor."

Ms. Peters, Mrs. Brown, and the Dickson's were present for the ceremony and all had tears of pride and joy on their faces as Faith received her award.

After the ceremony was over, Ella Mae Brown, John, and Ruth took Faith to lunch at The Hilltop House Restaurant, where Ruth shared some good news with her. Ruth said, "According to Carolyn Woodruff, our fabulous family attorney from Greensboro whom we hired to help us, it's possible that you could become our adopted daughter and come home with us sometime early next year." The Dickson's and Mrs. Brown then dropped her off at the orphanage and returned home to Wilmington.

***

It was rapidly becoming a beautiful new life for Faith! By this time, her weight had gotten down to less than one hundred and thirty pounds and was still going down, and she was looking absolutely great. She would arise early each morning and go for a two-mile run, and go for another one after dinner for two more miles. Despite this, she would still experience an occasional craving for a candy bar, which she would quickly reject because she knew this devil would always be lurking deep inside her psyche and looking for an opportunity to re-invade and retake control of her life.

The orphanage director, Ms. Sasser, gave Faith a compensated job at the orphanage to do housework and help take care of the smaller children. Faith would endorse her small weekly paychecks over to Mary Kay towards reimbursing her for that which Faith had taken from her several months earlier.

Faith took a special interest in the orphanage children who were overweight and/or handicapped, and developed some fun games with a spiritual theme for them to play that focused on building their confidence and self-esteem. Ms. Sasser was so impressed with the program that she highlighted Faith's work in her monthly report to the State Director. The program received many compliments and was replicated in several of the other orphanages within the State system.

Faith was enjoying every moment of her new life and was beginning to envision what her eventual role in life might be...perhaps as a psychologist or psychiatrist whose specialty would be to work with children who were suffering from the same terrible condition she once had! Although it seemed like an incredibly steep mountain for her to climb from where she was, she now had the fullest of confidence that it would someday happen!

***

Everything seemed to be going so well for Faith until late one evening when Ms. Sasser knocked on her bedroom door. When Faith opened it, the teary-faced director entered her bedroom and sadly said, "Please sit down, Faith. I'm afraid I have some very bad news to share with you."

"What is it, Ms. Sasser? Are you okay?"

Ms. Sasser said, "Yes honey, I'm okay, but the news I have to share with you breaks my heart and I know it will sadden you as well. I just received a phone call from your soon to be mom, Mrs. Dickson at Carolina Beach, who told me to let you know that your dear friend, Mrs. Ella Mae Brown from Wilmington, passed away last night.

Her funeral service will be held at the Beulah A.M.E. Church in Wilmington on the day after tomorrow. If you want to go there, I'll be glad to make arrangements for your transportation and clear it with your probation officer."

As Ms. Sasser put her arms around her, Faith began to softly cry. After a few moments of weeping, she wiped away her tears and asked the director if she would kneel and say a prayer for Mrs. Brown with her. Ms. Sasser knelt beside and joined her.

As Faith knelt beside her bed she prayed, "Dear

Heavenly Father, I know my very special friend, Mrs. Ella Mae Brown, is there in Heaven with you now. She is a dear friend, and I beg you to please give her my love and deepest thanks for playing such an important part in my life by getting me to know, follow, and love you. In Jesus' holy name I pray. Amen."

\*\*\*

The next morning, Faith was driven to the Fayetteville Bus Station by Ms. Sasser and boarded a Greyhound bus that would take her to Wilmington where John and Ruth would meet her. When she stepped off of the bus, they greeted her with mixed tears; sorrow over the loss of Ella Mae, and joy to have her with them. They then drove out to the Dickson's Carolina Beach home, which in Faith's mind was her *real* home.

When she placed the small bag of her things in her bedroom, she saw a beautiful dark blue dress hanging on the closet door and it was a size 10...a far cry from the 3X size she had been wearing less than a year ago!

Ruth walked into the room and said, "This pretty dress is for you to wear to the funeral tomorrow, honey, and I know it's going to fit you just right, you beautiful thing you. It belonged to our Christina and was one of her favorite dress-up things. You'll even look 'kinda like her with it on and there are some pretty matching shoes for it there under your bed."

Faith hadn't given any thought about what she would wear to the funeral, and was so pleased to have the dress, especially that it had been Ruth's *other* daughter's, and that she could actually fit into a size ten! She hugged Ruth and thanked her for being so thoughtful. She then tried on the pretty blue dress and it fitted her like a glove!

Ruth said, "Honey, you have no idea how proud I am to see you looking so great. How do you feel about you and me taking a little run on the beach together for old time's sake?"

Faith hung up the dress; then she and Ruth threw on their shorts and tennis shoes and headed out for the beach where they began walking and stretching for a few minutes, and then took off running.

As they ran, Ruth said, "Let me know when you get tired of running, Faith, and we'll stop."

Faith replied, "I'm running this one in Mrs. Brown's honor, Mom, so there'll be no stopping for me this time. I'll run until I drop."

To Ruth's amazement, Faith stayed with her all the way for the entire two mile run! When they returned to the Dickson home, Ruth said, "I can't believe you, girl! Why you nearly ran the legs off of me!"

Faith grinned and said, "You showed me how to do it, Mom, and I just couldn't let you and Mrs. Brown down."

After enjoying a nice dinner of grilled shark steaks that John, who was a great cook, had caught and prepared for them, everyone retired for the evening in preparation for the funeral early the next day.

*\*\*\**

When they arrived at the Beulah A.M.E. Church in Wilmington the next morning, they found it filled to capacity. Mrs. Brown's son, Jeremy, met them in front and tearfully said, "I know my Mom would be honored if you nice folks would sit up front with my Mom's family." Faith and the Dickson's thanked Jeremy and proudly sat in a front pew with the Brown family.

The service began with the beautiful singing of some

of Ella Mae's favorite hymns by the church choir. Faith was especially moved by Ella Mae's most favorite hymn, *Amazing Grace.*

Afterwards, Reverend Maurice Johnson, the same minister who had first uttered the words that would become Faith's personal inspirational motto, read from the twenty-third Psalm and spoke at great length about Ella Mae's faith, her many contributions to the life of the church, and how she had always set a wonderful example for others. He then asked for those who desired to come forward and offer their personal eulogies.

Several people, including the Mayor of Wilmington and the City's Chief of Police, came forward to praise Ella Mae's kindness and good works. When the long procession of people who gave their eulogies had finally ended, Faith stood and walked to the lectern to deliver her eulogy.

Without the use of notes, Faith began in an occasionally choking voice. "In the past year, several people have touched my life in such a deep and meaningful way by showing and encouraging me in the right way to live, and my beautiful friend, Mrs. Ella Mae Brown, was the person who started the process in me which resulted in my discovering the way, the truth, and the life with Jesus.

Please visualize in your minds a poor, frightened and severely obese fourteen-year-old girl who was running away from the many problems in her life, and was standing all alone in the rain on a lonely highway late at night. The girl neither knew where she was nor where she was going. She didn't even know for sure *who* she was.

A dear, sweet, and lovely lady by the name of Mrs. Ella Mae Brown, who was driving home to Wilmington in her old station wagon after having helped out a friend of hers in Fayetteville, stopped and offered this confused and angry young obese girl a ride.

What followed that ride began a life-changing series of miracles for this frightened and lost young girl. Mrs. Brown befriended her and introduced her to Jesus; and that introduction resulted in a transformation from the girl's being a lost soul to one with an entirely new and blessed life and an even better future.

I know these things that I just told you about happened, because I *am* that girl. Thank you, Mrs. Ella Mae Brown, for what you have done for me and for so many others, and may you enjoy your well-earned new life with Him whom you have loved in your earthly life, and who deeply loves you, your friend and thanks to you, now also mine, our Lord Jesus."

Everyone in the church was touched to tears by Faith's moving and beautifully delivered eulogy, and gave her a standing applause.

***

Later that afternoon, the Dickson's took Faith to the Wilmington Greyhound bus station for her return trip to Fayetteville and to what she considered as her *temporary* home at the orphanage.

When the bus arrived at the Fayetteville bus station late that night, Mary Kay was waiting for her. They returned to the orphanage and Faith went directly to bed.

During her sleep that night, Faith had a frightening nightmare. In it, she dreamed that she had returned to her old life of obesity and anger. She tossed and turned as she visualized herself stuffing her face with candy bars, becoming obese again and hating everyone around her...especially herself.

She awakened, shaking, crying, and feeling afraid for the first time in months, and immediately dropped to her knees in prayer. After saying her prayer asking for God's help, she was relieved that it was only a dream, but one which served to remind her that she still had many challenges and opportunities ahead of her to meet and it wasn't going to be an easy trip.

***

Now nearing the end of her sophomore year of high school and, although her life had incredibly improved, Faith would sometimes find herself feeling an irrational fear that she wouldn't be able to maintain the steady path of improvement that the past year had brought into her new and better life. When these feelings would enter her mind, she would mentally visualize Ella Mae Brown and her soon-to-be parents encouraging her, and the negative anxiety would leave.

The long-awaited good news from the Dickson's finally arrived! Ruth called Faith and told her that their Greensboro family attorney, Mrs. Carolyn Woodruff, had finally secured the court's permission to terminate the restrictions of her probation, and that the adoption process could now move forward.

As much as she had looked forward for this wonderful event to occur, the reality that she would have to change schools if she moved to Carolina Beach made her feel a little anxious because she was now doing so well at Terry Sanford High School, but she didn't want to bring it up to the Dickson's.

But when the Dickson's drove to Fayetteville on Friday to take her home to Carolina Beach with them for the weekend, they brought up the change of school issue with Faith.

Ruth said, "Honey, in just a few days you will officially become our daughter, a day for which we have all prayed for over a year. The only concern we now have is in doing what will be the best for you.

You have experienced a miraculous turnaround in your schoolwork in Fayetteville, and we would hate to risk interrupting this fantastic progress by transferring you to another school in Wilmington at this stage of your education. What are your thoughts on this important issue?"

Faith replied, "Mom, I hope you and Dad are half as happy as I am over my forthcoming adoption as your daughter, and I promise you that I will do all in my power to please you and make you proud of me. You have no idea how happy this has made me. You are right on about the school issue, and that's another example of why I love you so much...because you care about what's best for me.

There's no denying that things are going incredibly well for me at my school in Fayetteville and I really do enjoy it. But if I must make a choice between being with you two wonderful people and staying at my school in Fayetteville, there's no question...I want to be with you."

John injected, "Maybe there's an alternative we could look into, honey. We've thought about investing a little bit of inherited money that we've been sitting on in a savings account for a long while in some real estate. Suppose we buy us a second home in Fayetteville and spend our weekdays there, and our summers, holidays, and most weekends at our Carolina Beach home? Wouldn't that take care of both issues?"

Faith hugged his neck and said, "I love you so much, Dad!"

"Then that's what we're gonna do," said John.

"Tomorrow, I'll call Janie King who's a real estate broker and good friend of mine in Fayetteville, and see if she can find us a good deal on a home for us that's within walking distance of your school."

Faith was beside herself with joy and optimism, and promised herself that she would do everything in her power to make her parents be glad for their unselfish decision.

# Chapter Ten

The adoption of Faith by the Dickson's came off without a hitch and became official.

With her addiction to fattening food and compulsion towards inappropriate expressions of anger finally totally behind her, and now comfortably living with her wonderful adoptive parents in a beautiful new condominium on Fort Bragg Road in the historic Haymont section of Fayetteville that her dad had purchased for them, Faith's life couldn't have been better! Her school performance and achievements continued to soar in the years that followed in virtually every aspect of her life, and she soon found herself entering into her senior year of high school.

She had applied for admission to several colleges, but was unsure as to how she would be able to manage their expensive costs. John had pretty much emptied the family treasury in the purchase of their second home, and the Dickson's retirement income wasn't nearly enough to pay for the high cost of Faith's college expenses. John even offered to sell their dream home at Carolina Beach to support her costs for college, but Faith would have none of that.

Faith did some deep thinking and research into the matter and finally developed what seemed to be a workable plan. She decided she would find a job immediately after she graduated from high school and save all the money she could during the summer. In the fall, she would attend Fayetteville Technical Community College, which was a good school and the least expensive educational option, and then work towards obtaining an academic scholarship to one of the larger universities to pursue her third and fourth years and a bachelor's degree.

About a month before her graduation from Terry Sanford High School was to take place, Faith was called into the Principal's office where Ms. Peters and several of the department heads were gathered. When she entered the office, everyone stood up with smiling faces and the Principal said, "We're gathered here, Miss Thomas, to make a very important announcement that concerns you."

After a experiencing a brief negative flashback where Faith feared that she had done something wrong and was about to be punished by this group of important people, she politely asked, "what would that announcement be, sir?"

The Principal smiled and said, "The selection committee has concluded that you are the best qualified graduating student to serve as the graduating class Valedictorian. Will you accept this honor and important responsibility, Miss Thomas?"

Faith was stunned! *They want me to serve as the class valedictorian? That's impossible! Oh my God, I don't believe it!* She broke into tears and told the Principal she would gladly accept the honor, profusely thanked him and each of the committee members, and then prepared to leave the room.

The Principal said, "Just a minute, my dear, don't leave just yet. There's a lot more that comes with your selection as the class valedictorian. You will receive a full, four-year scholarship from a local anonymous donor to any accredited State university that you choose and will accept you as a student.

Through smiling tears, Faith gratefully thanked the Principal and the staff, and couldn't wait to return home to share this fantastic good news with her parents!

\*\*\*

She said a prayer of thanks and then excitedly ran home faster than she ever had; but when she arrived at the family home, she saw several emergency vehicles parked in front and wondered what in the world could be happening. When she attempted to enter the home, a fireman stepped in front of her and said, "I'm very sorry, Miss, but you can't go in there."

"What do you mean I can't go in there?" Faith asked in a loud and frustrated voice. "This is my home and my mom and dad are inside."

The Fire Department Chaplain stepped forward and said, "I'm so sorry to have to tell you, Miss Thomas, but your parents were both taken to the hospital just a few minutes ago. They were just around the corner when it seems that your father suffered a heart attack while driving home with your mother. He sideswiped a pickup truck and then hit a tree broadside on the passenger side, seriously injuring him and your mother. Fortunately, your father had enough strength to call 911 for help.

Your mom and dad are now at the Cape Fear Valley Medical Center and I understand they're both still alive and are receiving treatment. I'll be glad to take you to the hospital in my emergency vehicle to see them."

The Chaplain and Faith raced to the hospital in the emergency vehicle with its lights flashing. All the way there Faith prayed aloud, "Please Dear God, let me have my wonderful parents for awhile longer. I know that Dad is ninety-one and Mom is eighty-nine and have led blessed lives, but please, please, let me have a little more time with them if it is Your will."

The Chaplain called ahead to determine where John and Ruth were located, so they would be able to go directly to them in the intensive care unit. She was first taken to Ruth's room. Ruth was clearly a very sick woman who had an oxygen mask and several monitoring instruments attached to her, and she was awake but barely able to speak.

Through choking tears, Faith said, "Mom, please don't leave me now. You know I love you more than life and I still need you, my precious and beautiful running buddy."

In a very weak and shaky voice, Ruth lifted her oxygen mask and replied, "Don't worry, my sweet little running buddy, I'll never leave you, not ever. I'll always be here with you in my spirit, even when this old body of mine finally gives out and I have to leave this world. You know I'll be in Heaven with our God and always watching you while you enjoy the wonderful life you deserve.

If you really love me, honey, please don't cry over my leaving; instead, let us thank our dear Lord for giving us each other and live your life the way I know you will, and think of me each day when you take your runs because I'll always be with you...and no more candy bars, sweetheart!" After saying that, Ruth smiled, her eyes then slowly closed, and the alarms on the monitoring equipment to which she was connected began to sound.

Faith knelt beside the bed with Ruth's cold hand in hers and tearfully said, "Goodbye, my precious Mom, and please give Jesus my love. I know you're there with Him now and you know I will always love you." She then tearfully proceeded to John's room in the ICU.

John was still alive, though barely. When Faith took his hand in hers, his eyes slowly opened and he said in a weak voice, "It's my time to move on to the next life, my dear precious Faith. I hear your dear mother calling me so I'll have to be leaving you soon to be with her. I want you to know that she and I love you and we will both be watching you all of your life here until we're together again in Heaven; so you always keep on being the good girl that we're so proud of." His eyes then slowly closed and he was gone. Faith tearfully held his hand and said the same words to John that she had to Ruth.

Ms. Peters heard what had happened and went directly to Faith's home to console her. Although fearing the worst reaction from Faith, she was pleasantly surprised at how well she was coping with the loss of her beloved parents.

Faith said to her with a smile, "My dear mom and dad are now saints in another and much more beautiful life now, Ms. Peters. I will always miss and love them, but it's more important that I follow the wonderful example that they set for me. That's how I shall honor them every day for the rest of my life on Earth."

The Dickson's memorial service was held at their church in Wilmington, and was heavily attended and officiated by the Bishop of Eastern North Carolina. After the service was over, and in compliance with their wills, Faith took their ashes that were combined into one canister and spread them all along the beach route which they had run daily as she walked along and spoke with them.

She said, "Mom and Dad, I know these ashes are only symbolic of you because both of you, the real you, are enjoying the heavenly reward which you so richly deserve, a life that's as beautiful as you are with our best friend, Jesus. I will remember you every day for the rest of my life, especially when I run, and promise you that I will always stay by my commitment to you and myself to be all that I can be. I love you and look forward to our being together again one day, as I know we shall."

\*\*\*

A week later, the graduation exercises at Terry Sanford High School were held and the valedictory speech Faith gave was hailed as the most moving ever, and was published in several major newspapers, including *The New York Times, the Fayetteville Observer, the News and Observer,* and several others around the country.

After being introduced by the Principal, Faith said, "Ladies and gentlemen, distinguished members of our faculty, our honored guests, and my fellow graduates. As I stand before you, I feel as though I'm living a dream…a truly wonderful dream that has finally become a reality, and I am sure my entire graduating class is happily feeling the joy of this wonderful celebration with me.

Four years ago when I first entered this school, I was a completely lost soul…angry, fat, and with no purpose in mind for my future. I once even tried to run away from it, as I had from just about all the other challenges in my life. Some of you may know of my pathetic beginning here. I had no vision to drive me and had all but given up on my life ever amounting to anything worthwhile.

Then I met a wonderful lady whom I had known many years before, Ms. Cheryl Peters, a counselor for me and many of my classmates here at our school. Ms. Peters saw some good in me as she does in all of her students, and began a process that ultimately resulted in the honor of my being invited to speak to you today on behalf of my graduating class.

In my first day here, my homeroom teacher, Miss

Ploeger, asked each one in the class to describe our goals in life and, sadly, I had none. My only hope was to simply survive, rather than discover and meet the challenges and opportunities that lay ahead of me.

Through a steady stream of miraculous interventions, which ultimately led to more faith in myself by submitting to and following the wisdom of the highest power in my life, our Lord Jesus Christ, I am proud to say that I'm about to become a Terry Sanford High School graduate.

Now that's enough about me, but I especially wanted to share this personal experience with you, even though it might cause some of the church and state separation zealots some heartburn.

Today, as we bring one of the most important milestones in our lives to closure through this graduation ceremony, on behalf of my class mates, I salute the many wonderful people who have helped to shape and prepare each of us for the exciting and challenging future which we all now face.

High on the list of the wonderful people who have greatly influenced us are our terribly underpaid and highly dedicated teachers who have graciously provided all of us with the basic working tools we will need in order to continue in the growth of our knowledge and skills. We salute and deeply thank all of you great men and women for these wonderful gifts which you have provided for us.

In many ways, it is a troubled world into which all of us shall soon enter, and we can deal with it by whining about it and succumbing to its troubles, or we can view it as our responsibility to help make it change for the better. I like to think that we in this graduating class perceive our role as being in the latter by making a positive difference through how we approach the days and years that lie ahead of us.

119

Many of us have been blessed with the opportunity of furthering our education through attending a college or trade school; some of us will choose to serve our country by joining the military, and some will take whatever jobs we can find and do the best we can to live positive and honorable lives.

But whatever route we choose to pursue for our future, we can all do it with the comfort of knowing that we have a place out there for which we have been well prepared during our four years here at Terry Sanford High School, and it's now up to us to discover where that place is.

I'm reminded of the Army's old recruiting slogan, 'Be All You Can Be,' and that's what I pray we shall all aspire to do as we move forward from this important milestone in our lives and become all that we can be. Thank you and I pray that God will bless you, my fellow classmates and your families, as we set out to become all we can be."

Faith received a thundering standing applause as the Principal hugged her and handed her a diploma. In her mind, she could hear Ruth's voice saying, "Great job, honey... I can hear the applause all the way up here in Heaven!"

# Chapter Eleven

Faith's friends had suggested she sell at least one of the two properties in Fayetteville or Carolina Beach which she had inherited from the Dickson's and had considerable value; however, she chose to keep both of them, rent out the Carolina Beach home and live in the Fayetteville one...not that she couldn't use the money to help subsidize her in college, but these homes were like sacred memorials to her loving parents and which she could never bring herself to sell for any reason.

Faith applied to and was immediately accepted at Ruth's other daughter, Christina's, alma mater, the Methodist University in Fayetteville as a Psychology major. Her goal was to complete her bachelor's, master's and doctoral degrees in Psychology and then open a counseling clinic to initiate a program that focuses on the treatment of obesity and anger management in troubled and handicapped adolescents.

When she began her college career at Methodist University, she was invited to pledge by several national sororities, including Beta Omicron Zeta, whose members were generally not as well off nor as physically attractive as most members of the other sororities, and a large number of the sisters were overweight...and that's the sorority that Faith chose to join.

She also went out for and made the girls' basketball team and wrote a column on fitness for the University's student newspaper. Faith was determined to approach college as she had high school, by striving to be all she could be. She also made a regular daily morning and evening run in honor of her deceased mother and father.

Late in her junior year at Methodist, Faith met a young man in one of her classes whom she found interesting and charming. Thomas "Tommy" Jordan was a friendly and bright young gentleman with a great sense of humor and was also an excellent student. Although Tommy was pretty handsome, he was a little overweight. He and Faith met while they were working together in a study group for one of her psychology courses and they quickly became real good buddies.

One day after class, Tommy invited Faith to join him for lunch at the K & W cafeteria in Fayetteville, which she accepted. As they were going through the serving line, Faith was shocked at the amount and types of food Tommy had placed on his tray. He had a double order of mashed potatoes that was loaded with thick gravy, Bar-B-Q pork, corn bread, a large slice of lemon meringue pie, and his beverage was a large glass of Mountain Dew soda.

Without giving any thought to his feelings, she impulsively and tactlessly said, "Good gosh, Tommy, you've got enough food on your tray to feed a family of four and it's all so darned unhealthy and fattening. Do you really need to eat that much and that kind of junky stuff?"

Tommy didn't take well to Faith's criticizing comment and snapped back at her that she should mind her own business and stay out of his. "You just don't understand, Faith, that we all have different appetites for food and mine just happens to be a little larger than yours, so please get the heck off of my back and stop lecturing me."

Faith continued, "Tommy, you know that I care for you as a friend and, as your friend, I feel obligated to warn you that you're on a pretty dangerous path with those kinds of food choices because they could put you on the road toward morbid obesity. Believe me, I know what I'm talking about because I've been to the awful place where your eating is going to take you if you don't get it under control soon, and I promise you're not gonna like it."

Tommy's normally friendly personality suddenly turned to outright anger and he snapped back, "Faith, I'd just as soon you either shut up or eat at another table, because I won't be able to enjoy my lunch with your criticizing and lecturing me like that about something that's none of your damned business." He then abruptly went to a different table where there was only one seat open, sat down, rapidly ate his lunch, and then angrily left the cafeteria alone.

Faith realized that, although she was correct in what she said, she shouldn't have said what she did to Tommy in such a put down and know-it-all manner. She recalled how she had felt during her obesity days when well-meaning people would criticize her for her food choices. This event was a valuable lesson learned for Faith, although it initially resulted in the loss of her valued friendship with Tommy.

She began to make notes of lessons she would learn from these experiences of communicating with people who were suffering from obesity. She intended to someday put these lessons learned into a guide for her use and to share with others who were working with obese people.

The first entry in Faith's notebook was: *Do not remind obese people that their eating is unhealthy and they*

*need to lose weight, because they probably know it quite
well... unless they're just stupid or crazy, which few are.
Instead, encourage <u>them</u> to bring it up and discuss it an
understanding way rather than criticizing or reminding
them that they have a problem. It's like telling an amputee
that he or she is missing a limb!* From that initial entry
into Faith's notebook, many pages would follow, which
she aspired to perhaps put into a book one day.

As stated earlier, some of the girls in Faith's sorority
were far from being beauty queens, and several were
chubby to obese and were of a special interest to Faith.
Not long after joining the sorority, Faith started a fitness
group with those girls that quickly produced impressive
results, with the average individual weight loss among
the fifteen overweight girls being around twenty-five
pounds! By the time her freshman year ended, her
sorority's image had rapidly changed from having the
least attractive to some of the most attractive young
ladies on the campus!

Faith's criticism of her friend, Tommy's, eating habits
at the cafeteria had resulted in an estrangement of their
once very close and enjoyable friendship. She called his
phone and left messages several times with no reply, and
even sent him a note of apology for criticizing him, to
which he also didn't respond.

Put bluntly, Tommy made it quite clear that he was
thoroughly pissed off at Faith for her well-intentioned but
highly offensive remarks about his eating habits!

One evening while walking back to her dormitory, she
accidentally ran into Tommy. They were in such close
proximity to each other on the sidewalk that something
had to be said, even if it was only a nod or wave. She
observed that he had gained at least thirty or more
pounds during the three-month termination of their
communications and was looking quite chubby.

Tommy looked at her and said, "Hi, Faith, it's good to see you again. I'll bet you didn't recognize me with all this extra blubber hanging on me, did you?"

Faith replied, "It's good to see you, too, Tommy, and of course I recognize you. I've really missed our times together. How have you been?"

In a sad and depressed voice, Tommy said, "To be honest with you, I've been pretty miserable, Faith, and I've really missed our friendship. In fact, I'm kind of embarrassed that we ran into each other because I didn't want you to see me looking as fat as I've allowed myself to become. And you sure were right when you said what you did to me that day in the cafeteria, because I've really become a fat slob like you predicted I would, haven't I?"

Faith smiled warmly and replied, "No, Tommy, you're not a fat slob. You're a very fine man and my good friend, and I've really missed you a lot."

Tommy's eyes began to fill with tears and he replied, "You really do still think of me as your friend even though I've insulted you by ignoring your several calls, and letting my body turn to pure shit?"

Faith said, "Tommy, I never judged you by your body weight or what you looked like on the outside, but by what's inside you...your character and intellect, and you're one of the healthiest and smartest guys I've ever known in those areas. I think of you as a really good friend and only want to help you to care for yourself. If you're unhappy with your body, there are things you can do to change it if you feel you really want to, and I'll be very glad to work with you to help you make it happen."

As they began to walk together, she said, "There are some things about me that you don't know, Tommy. A few years ago I had a very serious weight problem; in fact, when I was only fourteen years old, I weighed even more than you do now and everyone judged me by my then very fat body, without giving any consideration to what kind of a person I was inside. I was one very angry and unhappy girl until some wonderful things happened in my life that caused me to change."

Tommy replied, "You're kidding me, Faith. That's quite a story and hard for me to believe that you of all people have ever been obese. Whatever you might have been before, you're one of the prettiest girls on this campus now so why in the world would you want to have anything to do with a guy like me who's a fat slob and such a damned hypersensitive hothead?"

"Because you're a smart fellow, Tommy, you have a good sense of humor, you're a handsome guy, and, most of all, you've become one of my dearest friends...that's why," Faith replied.

From that conversation on, Tommy and Faith became nearly inseparable, and he also became her daily running buddy. A few months later, a now physically fit Tommy made the University's tennis team as a walk-on! He and Faith regularly worked out in the gym together, attended church together, and took an active role as volunteers at the University's Student Health Center where they would assist overweight students with motivational counseling and workouts.

One Sunday after they had attended church together and were walking back to their dormitories, Tommy asked, "Faith, do you think you might someday see me as more than just a good friend? I'm sort of embarrassed to tell you this but I have to be honest and let you know that over the past year I can't help it but I've fallen head over heels in love with you."

Tommy's statement initially caused something resembling a flashback for Faith of her past experience with Wally, but she quickly separated the connection in her mind and, after a brief pause said, "I think I'm beginning to feel the same way about you as well, Tommy."

They briefly stared into each other's eyes, and then their lips touched for the first time. It wasn't a sloppy, hard, and lust-driven kiss like the one she had with Wally, but a soft and deeply felt one for both of them.

Tommy and Faith simultaneously softly said to each other, "I love you," and then shared a good laugh over the spontaneity of their statements.

Tommy then smilingly asked, "Then where do you think we go from here now that we've finally kissed each other, Faith?"

She replied, "Where we've pretty much been all along, as each other's dearest friend...I guess we can call it 'going steady'. While we're talking so seriously about the love stuff, I might as well tell you up front that I've made a vow that there will be no sexual intimacy for me until after I'm married and that can't be until after I graduate.

A guy once raped me when I was only fourteen and that really scarred my thoughts about sex before marriage. That's a serious commitment that I've made to myself and I will not violate it for any reason. Does hearing this bother you, Tommy, or make you want to change your mind about us?"

Tommy said, "No, Faith, it doesn't bother me at all. I understand your position, and I'll be happy to wait for that until if and when we should choose to be married because just having you as my best friend is worth more than any other pleasure I know."

"Should I interpret that to be a tentative marriage proposal, Tommy?" Faith asked.

Tommy replied, "Yep, I think you could say that."

"Then ask me again after we graduate and I'll give you an answer," Faith said with a giggle.

\*\*\*

During the campus-wide election, Faith was unanimously elected as the University's Homecoming Queen and was also elected to serve as the Vice President of the student body. She had become somewhat of a celebrity at the University, and was even persuaded to participate in the Miss North Carolina Pageant in Wilmington, where she was the first runner up.

After an outstanding four years of undergraduate work, Faith and Tommy both graduated *magna cum laude* with bachelor's degrees in Psychology and they both immediately entered into a graduate program at the University of North Carolina at Pembroke to earn their master's degrees in psychology.

By this time, Faith had become somewhat of a celebrity around the entire state, often appearing on regional television talk shows on behalf of a foundation that she and Tommy were creating together to help young people in their fight against obesity. Tommy was the son of a prominent Raleigh doctor of internal medicine who assisted them in forming the foundation and also served as its medical advisor.

Tommy's parents, Dr. and Mrs. Michael Jordan, invited Faith to join them for dinner one night at the very posh Quail Hollow Country Club in Raleigh. Faith hadn't yet met Tommy's mother and was eagerly looking forward to it.

When Faith met Mrs. Jordan, a very attractive and well dressed lady in her early fifties, Mrs. Jordan was very charming and gracious. She said, "I've heard so many nice things about you from my husband and son,

Faith, and I'm so glad we've finally been able to meet. Are you related to the Dr. Richard Thomas who has a pediatric clinic in Fayetteville? His lovely wife, Margaret, and I made our debuts together at the Cotillion several years ago."

Faith told Mrs. Jordan that she wasn't related to him and, as far as she knew, she had no living relatives. From that point on, Mrs. Jordan's previous warmth and charm seemed to chill a bit, especially when Faith let her know that she had lived in an orphanage for much of her earlier life. Her attitude towards Faith quickly shifted from being warm and friendly to aloof and coldly polite. Mrs. Jordan was clearly unimpressed with Faith's socially classless background.

Faith and Tommy spent much of their off-duty and vacation time in providing lectures on personal health management and counseling to high school students around the state. Faith was especially pleased to be invited to speak to the students at Terry Sanford High School, where Cheryl Peters had been promoted and was now serving as its Principal.

When Faith walked into Cheryl's office, it was a heartwarming reunion. After Faith introduced Tommy to her and they had spoken for a while, Cheryl whispered to Faith, "Where did you find this fantastic young man, Faith? You two are going to be married one day, aren't you?"

Faith blushed and whispered back, "I hope so, but we can't even think about something like that right now, Ms. Peters, because we're so darned busy with our schooling and work; but we sure are the best of friends and you'll be among the first to know if and when that happens."

Their presentation to the students received a standing ovation, and several students who were suffering from obesity signed up for an on line workshop that was designed by Faith and Tommy to motivate them away from their unhealthy lifestyles and into a new and much healthier one.

After the presentation in Fayetteville was over, Faith and Tommy made the drive to Wilmington to make a similar presentation at a high school there.

As they passed through the small town of Tar Heel, Faith was mentally recalling the torment that she had experienced there many years earlier. She shared with Tommy all of the morbid details of the experience she had with Wally, over eight years before, including pointing out the small trailer park where she and Wally had stayed on that horrible night. After sharing her experience with Tommy, she asked, "Does hearing my disgusting story affect your feelings toward me, Tommy?"

Tommy replied, "Your honesty only makes me love you more, knowing how difficult it was for you and how far you had to climb in order to become the beautiful woman that you are today, Faith."

Faith asked, "What about the sex part, the fact that I had sex with another man when I was at such a young age, regardless of the circumstances? Doesn't it make you feel jealous or angry towards me, especially after I've taken the position with you of no sex until after marriage? It sorta makes me seem like a hypocrite, doesn't it?"

Tommy took her hand and said, "No, honey, it's just the opposite. I deeply sympathize with you and understand that what happened to you wasn't something of your choice...you were the victim of some horrible circumstances which were beyond your control. By the way, I'd prefer that you not let my mother know anything about that period of your life, though.

You've probably already noticed how socially conscious she is and this kind of information could become a barrier to you all having a good relationship. Incidentally, my dear, beautiful Faith, I've been meaning to ask you an important question."

"What's that, honey?"

Tommy pulled the car over to the side of the road and stopped; then got out of the car and opened Faith's door. He knelt down on the ground before her and asked, "Will you marry me, Faith?"

Faith dropped to her knees on the ground beside him, put her arms around his neck and smilingly said, "Yes, Tommy, I will!"

Tommy then reached into his pocket and pulled out a beautiful five karat diamond engagement ring set in platinum that had been his deceased maternal grandmother's, and slipped it on Faith's finger. Faith stared at the beautiful ring and marveled at its unique beauty as they shared their thoughts about wedding plans for the remainder of their journey to Wilmington.

Tommy said he felt they should have a large, formal wedding at his family's church in Raleigh to satisfy his family and especially his very social conscious mother, but Faith said she leaned toward a small private ceremony. Tommy's comment about his mother's preference was the only slightly negative thought in her otherwise happy mind.

They agreed they would wait to set a date until after they completed their master's degrees and had a chance to review their calendar of future commitments to determine the most convenient date and place to schedule it.

Faith said, "I've got to focus my thinking on our presentation that'll be starting in just an hour, Tommy, but we can talk more about the wedding afterwards. The Carolina Beach house is vacant this weekend, so let's stay over there tonight rather than driving back to Fayetteville so late at night so we can talk."

# Chapter Twelve

When Faith and Tommy arrived in Wilmington, they went directly to the Holiday Inn where a large group of local health care professionals and several members of the public awaited them in a large conference room.

Faith stood behind the podium and began the presentation. "Welcome, ladies and gentlemen, and thank you for joining us for this event. We hope that what we have to share with you professionals will be of value to you in your work with those who are suffering from obesity, and that those of you who suffer from it will become motivated to overcome it and be all you can be.

As you know, obesity is a widespread and a potentially very dangerous and debilitating disorder, and one that my colleague, Tommy, and I are committed to do all we can to help people deal with and overcome.

As to our credentials, we are both completing our master's degrees in psychology at the University of North Carolina at Pembroke, and our future plans call for expanding our foundation's program throughout our state and, we hope, someday across the entire country." She went into a description of current thinking, including several of the most popular theories related to obesity, with statistics and nicely done diagrams that were projected on to a large overhead screen.

*Edward Vaughn*

"Our most significant credential regarding this topic isn't a scholarly one, though, but more of an *experiential* one. Tommy and I were once both suffering from obesity and struggled with it for many years until we discovered that there are no easy, simple, and quick ways to extricate ourselves from this horribly disabling disorder.

Every time I would go on the Internet, I would find it bombarded with numerous quick-fix instant remedies for obesity. They include all sorts of pills, gadgets, and some of the most ridiculous diets imaginable.

One such ridiculous diet I recently read even called for swallowing dried honey bees! Of course, they cost $39.99 per container, plus around ten bucks for shipping and handling, and one would be expected to take them indefinitely...and they would then sell your personal and credit card information to another scam operator to further use you! Their common denominator is that virtually none of them work for anyone except those who profit financially from their deceptive scams.

The simple matter of fact is that nothing will work until those who suffer from this awful condition reach the point where they are willing to do something - something that is somewhat uncomfortable to many people but works - and that something is to commit to and religiously follow a major change in how they live their lives and follow it with inspired action!

This simple something also requires that they cease in their denial and see themselves as they really are, and then make a deep commitment towards a major change in how they live their lives. The rest is a no-brainer that only requires major dietary changes and lots of physical exercise.

Some of you may disagree, but we believe that the next step once that commitment is made but often delayed indefinitely is, as Nike says, "Just do it!"

The 'it' to which I am referring is simply *eating the right foods and engaging in an appropriate amount of physical exercise*...then your body and your positive thinking brain will pretty much take care of the rest."

She described the physiology and psychology of obesity in detail, pointing out that the types of food people ingest and the use of their bodies are basically the essence of what produce the outcomes, good or bad.

Faith received a standing ovation for her well-designed and delivered presentation.

After their formal two-hour group presentation was over, Faith and Tommy made themselves available in a private room for individual consultations.

Faith's first individual consultation was with Sylvia O'Brian, a moderately obese lady who appeared to be in her early forties and who, at first, was polite and seemed interested in speaking with Faith.

Faith assumed it was about giving Sylvia some guidance towards helping her with her personal weight situation; however, once they began their conversation, it quickly became a déjà vu of Faith's earlier experiences with her birth mother, Rebecca, which was fraught with anger.

After listening to Faith address some matters related to her condition for a few minutes, Sylvia suddenly exploded! "You arrogant bitch, what right do you have to be spreading the idea that all overweight people are bad? You're the kind of person who gives everyone the impression that there's something wrong with people who are a little overweight and that everyone should be a skinny, "Twiggy" type like yourself.

For your information, young lady, I happen to be a very successful businesswoman and have a happy marriage, and I've always been a little overweight by your ridiculously unrealistic standards."

Faith asked, "Then why are you here at the conference, Sylvia, and what is it that you want to discuss with me?"

"I'm here only because my husband suggested that I might find it interesting and it wound up only pissing me off," replied Sylvia.

"So why do you think your husband thought this presentation would be of interest to you?" Faith asked.

Sylvia angrily replied, "Don't you try to play your mind games on me, young lady. My husband has always thought I look great and has said so ever since we were first married."

Faith asked, "How long have you been married, Sylvia?"

"For eleven years," Sylvia replied.

"Do you have any children, Sylvia?"

"No, we don't have children, and what the hell has that got to do with anything?" Sylvia indignantly asked.

Faith asked, "How often do you and your husband engage in intimate relations, Sylvia?"

"That's a very personal matter and it's none of your damned business to ask me such a rude question...and it doesn't have anything to do with my body type!" Sylvia indignantly replied.

Faith then said, "Sylvia, I do sympathize with you because I've been where you seem to be and my input isn't likely to change your denial thinking about your weight problem unless you believe you have one."

"Problem?" replied Sylvia. "I don't have a damned problem."

Faith asked, "Then why did you ask to speak with me?"

Sylvia said, "Because...because I'm..." She stopped and put her hands over her face, and then broke out into choking sobs. "It's because I'm fat, damnit, a fat pig, and my husband hasn't even touched me for over three years. Now does that answer satisfy you?"

Faith gently took Sylvia's hand and kindly said, "Congratulations, Sylvia. You just took the first big step towards a healthier and prettier you by recognizing and *admitting* that you have a problem. Your husband must love you a whole lot to have suggested this instead of doing what a lot of other husbands do by going outside the marriage for their physical satisfaction. What size dress do you now wear, Sylvia?"

"It's like a damned tent, a size 18, and it's even getting too tight" Sylvia replied.

Faith said, "Sylvia, do you know you could be wearing a size 8 within ten months if you really want to? By the way, would you believe that I once wore a size dress that was even larger than yours...a whopping size 3X! You can do it, Sylvia, and it's not as difficult to do as you might think."

Sylvia cried as Faith gently held her hand and again said, "You can do it, Sylvia...you can be the beautiful and healthy woman that you want to be if you'll just follow the simple instructions listed in this little folder that I'm going to give you. I'm also going to give you my cell phone number which you're free to call any time you want to talk with me, and I will pray for your success."

Sylvia thanked her profusely and left with the folder of information Faith had given her and a smile and happy tears on her previously angry face. Faith and Tommy had over a dozen individual consultations with various types of men and women who had many different concerns related to the treatment of their obesity.

After their very successful individual conferences were concluded, Faith and Tommy drove out to Carolina Beach to stay at the beach house Faith had inherited from her deceased adoptive parents.

They went to dinner at the same restaurant where Faith had been arrested nearly ten years before. Ironically, the same lady that had turned Faith in to the police then was still working there at the cash register; but she didn't recognize Faith, who was now nearly eighty pounds lighter than she had been then.

Their lengthy discussion during a long walk on the beach following dinner was to become another major pivotal point in Faith and Tommy's lives. As they walked hand in hand along the beach, they talked at great length, mainly about how well things had gone at the presentation and about the future of their new Foundation.

Tommy finally stopped walking and asked, "Can't we take a break from talking about business issues, Faith? When are we going to get around to talking about and making some firm plans for our wedding?"

Faith replied, "I guess now is as good a time as any, Tommy. How about let's you and I just run away and get married, rather than go through all the unnecessary fuss of putting together a traditional big social show that will cost your parents and us a bundle of money and interrupt our work? Maybe we could go away on a cruise ship or something and be married by the ship's Captain while we're out at sea. I think that would be a 'kinda fun, very romantic, and practical way for us to do it."

Tommy said, "You're probably right, Faith, but my pretty large and socially prominent family will be expecting us to have what you call a traditional big show...especially my mother who, as you know, is very social conscious."

Faith snapped back with, "Whose wedding is it anyhow, hers or ours? And do I have any say so about what we do or is your mother going to be making our decisions about this and who knows what else for the rest of our lives?"

"Of course it's ours, but our families will want to

participate in such an important social event," replied Tommy. "I can't help it if my mother is so social conscious because that's just the way she is and I can't and won't try to change it."

Faith replied, "I know but I don't have to like it, though. As I've told you before, I have no family, Tommy...not one single person do I know that I'm related to. My mother was an only child and she's dead, and I don't even know if my father has any living relatives. And to be frank with you, all of this social stuff that concerns your mother is a lot of phony crap as far as I'm concerned. In fact, to be honest with you, I don't like her snobbish thinking because it makes me want to puke."

Tommy snapped back, "Now wait a minute, Faith; my mother is very dear to me whether or not you approve of her, so please don't say disparaging things about her. Heck, you've only met her once and I thought she was very nice to you."

"I'd call it condescending rather than nice, and she's made it quite clear to me that I'm not up to her high social standards," Faith haughtily replied. "I'm sure she would have preferred that you marry a debutante, or the daughter of someone who belongs to her snobby little country club."

As the issue of his family was being discussed, Tommy and Faith were becoming increasingly feisty towards each other. Finally, Faith said, "I think we're allowing ourselves to get too worked up and need to stop this discussion before we really piss each other off, Tommy. The bottom line is that you and I are from two different worlds on the family issue. I'm going to have to give a lot more thought about that part of the marriage issue before we can proceed with it any further."

Tommy angrily replied, "Then you suit yourself, Faith. I think I'd like to walk by myself for a while if you don't mind. This conversation isn't doing either of us any good and I think we both need a little time alone before one of us says something we might later regret."

Tommy angrily jerked his hand away from Faith's and started walking away from her in the opposite direction.

As she walked alone, barefooted and up to her knees in the ocean water, Faith thought to herself, *Am I getting myself into something by marrying Tommy that's not going to be right for either of us or interfere with my major goals in life? He and his family are so caught up in this socially proper stuff that I don't think I'll ever be comfortable with them, and I'm beginning to sense that he's more of a mama's boy than I realized.*

She began to pray: *Please, dear Jesus, help me calm my anger and guide me in the right direction. I know I love Tommy and he's a really good person; but maybe it would be wrong for us to marry and wind up fighting about his mother. Please help me make up my mind and do that which is right for both of us and I will do whatever You tell me to do.*

Suddenly a large wave crashed around her that knocked her down into the ocean. When she stood up, dripping wet, she said, "Thank you, Jesus, for giving me what I'm going to interpret as Your answer to my prayer."

She then walked back to the house where she found Tommy sitting alone and, something she had never seen him do, smoking a cigarette on the front porch of Faith's beach home. "Where the hell have you been for so long?" he angrily asked.

"I've been doing some very deep thinking, Tommy, and I think I'm going to have to pass on our marriage for now. I don't mean to hurt you, but I don't think it's going to work for us in the long haul." She then handed him back the beautiful engagement ring that he had placed on her finger only a few hours earlier.

Through choking tears, Tommy asked, "Why, Faith? Why are you doing this to me? You know that you're breaking my heart with your attitude, especially about how you regard my mother who's never been unkind to you."

Faith took his hand and said, "Tommy, it's tearing at my heart, too, because I do love you, but only as a dear friend and not as a husband. I'm sorry, but I'm just not ready for that yet.

You have your family that you adore, and I envy you for that since I don't have one. But I believe we would both be making a big mistake to marry because you would be the one who would suffer the most by being caught between your family's values and mine on some issues where we are a hundred and eighty degrees apart. Our differences would only become exacerbated over time by your trying to appease both of us and that wouldn't be fair to you."

Tommy asked, "Is this your final decision, Faith? Can't we at least discuss it further together and see if there's a way that we can work it out?"

"No, Tommy. It is a final decision and one of the most painful ones I've ever had to make. I have a calling in my life, and don't believe I can even consider marriage to you or anyone else until I accomplish some goals that I can't allow to be diluted by investing my mental energy into what I see as an irresolvable conflict."

"Okay, Faith, if that's your final decision, then I will leave you now and you can also consider our plans for the Foundation that we both dreamed of building together as going down the drain as well," Tommy angrily replied. Faith reached out to hug him goodbye and he quickly turned away from her, called for a taxi, then silently packed up his things and left.

Although it nearly crushed Faith's heart to make such a painful decision, it also gave her a feeling of relief. She knelt and gave thanks to God for giving her the courage to do what she knew had to be done, and asked God to be there for Tommy in the healing of his pain.

The old urge for a candy bar suddenly entered into her mind for a fleeting moment, but she quickly decided to go for a run on the beach to get rid of it. As she ran, she felt that she could hear Ruth's voice saying to her, "Although you're hurting over it right now, my little running buddy, you've made the right decision and this too shall pass. Don't give up your dream, Sweetie."

# Chapter Thirteen

Despite the sadness she was feeling from her earlier unpleasant episode with Tommy, Faith slept better that night than she had in several weeks. She arose at five a.m. and went for another run on the beach, and felt even better afterwards. She then loaded her things into her car, secured the beach home, and headed back to her home in Fayetteville.

She knew she needed to talk with someone she trusted to help her work through her still ambivalent feelings she had about not marrying Tommy, bring clarity to her thoughts, obtain final closure, and form a new plan to achieve her goals in life since doing the Foundation thing with Tommy and his father would probably be finis if she didn't marry him.

She called Cheryl Peters at the school and asked if she would join her for dinner that night, which Cheryl accepted. They met at the elegant Hilltop House Restaurant where they enjoyed a fabulous dinner and, rare for both of them, a glass of fine wine.

After dinner, they chatted at length with "small talk," and Cheryl asked, "Faith, tell me what's going on with you and Tommy. You haven't mentioned him once all evening. Are you two planning on getting married any time soon?"

Faith replied, "That's not going to happen, Cheryl...I'm afraid it's all over with us," and brought Cheryl up to date on the relationship conflict between her and Tommy.

Cheryl expressed her condolences and said, "If you aren't absolutely sure about marrying him, Faith, then you certainly did the right thing. As the old saying goes, 'if you marry in haste then you will repent at leisure.' Will this breakup have any effect on the project that you've been working on together?"

"I'm not sure right now how it'll be affected, Cheryl, because we haven't spoken since he left me at the beach last night; but if his snobby mommy has anything to do with it, it's all over with for me," replied Faith.

"If that's the case, what will this do to your future plans, Faith?"

Faith replied, "I suppose I'll have to develop a new plan if Tommy is serious about choosing to drop out and take away his father's important financial and medical advisory support, which wouldn't surprise me at all. Either way, I intend to continue in my determination to be all I can be with my dream of helping obese people in finding a way out of their nightmarish lives, and I won't let anything interfere with that."

Cheryl said, "I have to admire your determination, Faith, and I'm sorry things aren't going well in your love life. Please let me know if I can help you in any way." They hugged goodbye, and Faith returned home.

When she walked into her house, she checked her telephone voice mail. When she clicked on the first message, a voice said, "Faith, it's Wally Cochran. I know you probably don't want to hear from me after the terrible situation I put you through many years ago. But if you are willing, I would deeply appreciate the opportunity of talking with you.

Since that awful time in our lives, I spent three years

in the State prison before being paroled a few years ago, which I deserved for what I did to you and others; but after that was over, many good things have happened in my life. If you would be willing to speak with me, please call me back; but if you prefer not to, I will understand and won't bother you again."

Faith was shocked and confused in receiving this message from a man who had once essentially raped her and spoke of planning to kill her. She thought to herself, *Call him back? This guy has to be totally nuts to think, of all people, I'd ever want to talk with him again after what he did to me!*

She was both frightened and angry over hearing his voice again, and felt as though her life was beginning to fall apart. First, the upsetting breaking up with Tommy, and now hearing from the most horrible man she had ever known. She decided to go for a run and try to shake off the anxious and angry feelings that were controlling her thoughts.

While running, she again heard the voice of Ruth in her head. "Honey, I think you should go ahead and call Wally back. There has to be a reason for his calling. Maybe it's a good one, as impossible as it may seem to you now." In her mind, she replied to Ruth, "No way, Jose!"

When she returned from her run, her anxiety level had somewhat lowered and she was thinking more calmly and rationally. Her feelings about the call from Wally had shifted from anger and fear to plain curiosity. She continued to wonder why, of all people, he had called her. After saying her nightly prayers, she crawled into her bed and tried to fall asleep.

As hard as she tried, though, she could not stay asleep because she kept wondering why Wally had the audacity to have called her. Finally, near midnight, she decided she had to know why he was calling. She picked up the phone and dialed the number he had left on her voice mail.

A voice recording stated, "This is St. Alfred's Episcopal Church in Elizabethtown. All staff members have left for the day. If you wish to leave a message, please do so at the tone. If this is an emergency, please call 911 or call Reverend Cochran at 910-323-2875."

"*Reverend* Cochran?" Faith shouted loudly. "Oh my God, I can't believe it!" Without thinking about what time it was, she immediately dialed the number for Reverend Cochran and he answered on the first ring.

He recognized her phone number on his caller ID and said, "Faith, thank you so much for returning my call. I know it must have been upsetting for you to hear my voice again after the nightmare that I put you through about ten years ago. How are you?"

Faith was in a state of shock and at a loss for words. "I'm doing quite well, thank you. Are you really a *minister* now?"

"Yes, Faith, as much as I'm sure it shocked you to hear it, I really am. While I was in prison, I received some wonderful psychotherapy and what I call *theotherapy*, and was introduced to God through Jesus, and what followed that meeting is nothing short of a miracle. I became so committed to restructuring my life from the evil and meaningless one I had been leading and, as the Army used to say, 'to be all I can be,' that I entered the seminary shortly after my release from prison nearly eight years ago.

I'm serving in my first assignment as the assistant rector at St. Alfred's Episcopal Church in Elizabethtown, which is only about forty miles from Fayetteville, and I may be assigned to pastor another church somewhere else in the Eastern Diocese of North Carolina within the year.

The one thought that has never left me, Faith, is the deep regret I've lived with for the awful things I did to you many years ago. I recently read about your work with obese people in our Diocesan newsletter and couldn't believe it. As hard as it was for me to muster up the courage to do so, because I didn't want to upset you, I had to call you and tell you how proud I am of what you've accomplished in your life."

Faith was so awestruck in hearing the voice of a man who had once essentially raped her and said he was going to kill her, and who was now a Christian minister that she didn't know what to say, so she simply hung up the telephone.

She was torn between wanting to believe and forgive him, and wipe the memory of what had happened from her mind...and in not speaking with him at all ever again.

The thought of Wally being an ordained minister in the church was mind blowing to Faith. *This creepy, thieving, and conniving rapist is now a man of the cloth... ridiculous!* Her old urge to eat something fattening and sweet suddenly returned and was nearly overwhelming; so she did her usual thing when those feelings would enter into her mind and, despite the strange hour for it, went for another run, a long and speedy run.

As she ran, she was recalling that horrible night in Tar Heel and allowing her anger to take over her body and mind. She finally stopped in a park, got down on her knees, and prayed. "Dear Lord, what would You have me do? Forgive him for the awful things he did or never speak to him again? Please, Lord, tell me what I should do..."

She thought of the words from the Lord's Prayer, "As

we forgive those who trespass against us." She then knew what she had to do...call him and forgive him, just as Mary Kay and several others had done for her sins against them.

***

Trembling, Faith dialed Wally's - Reverend Cochran's- telephone number. She hadn't thought about the fact that it was nearly two in the morning when she did it, but Wally immediately answered on the first ring, indicating that he was also still awake.

"Thank you for calling me back, Faith. I know my call must have come as a real shock to you."

Faith replied, "Yes, it really did, Wally, and I apologize for returning the call so late and hanging up on you the way I did. I just didn't know what to say to you. In the name of Jesus, I forgive you for your past transgression toward me, and hope you will extend the same to me for my trying to kill you."

Wally said, "You were more than justified in what you did to me then, Faith, and owe me no apology. I know I have no right to ask it of you, but I would deeply appreciate the opportunity of expressing my apology to you face-to-face if that would be possible.

I have to be in Fayetteville next Sunday to fill in for the rector, Father Robert Alves, at St. John's Episcopal Church as what we call a supply priest while he's attending a Diocesan conference in Wilmington. Is there any chance that you and I could meet for lunch after the service?"

Faith paused and remained quiet for several seconds.

Wally broke the silence and asked, "Are you still there, Faith?"

148

"Yes, Wally, I am. I just don't know what to do. One side of me would be very glad to see you, if you are for real, but I have to be honest and tell you that my memories of the past are making it very difficult."

"I do understand your feelings on the matter, Faith. Why don't you give it as much time as you need to think it over and not give me an answer right now? It would be wonderful for me if I should see you at the church on Sunday, but will understand if you choose not to be there. Will that work for you?" Wally asked.

Faith replied, "That's fine, and I appreciate your kind and understanding words, Wally. I know it wasn't easy for you to call me." She then said goodbye and hung up the phone but stayed awake for most of the night thinking about this strange event.

\*\*\*

The following Sunday morning, Faith got out of bed early because she couldn't sleep, took a shower, and got dressed. She spent over an hour debating with herself as to whether or not she should go to the church where Wally—now Reverend Cochran—would be leading the service which was to begin at 10:30 a.m.

At 10:15, she finally decided to go. She got into her car and drove down Green Street to St. John's Episcopal Church. She waited in the narthex of the church until the service began, and then quietly slipped into one of the rear pews.

When Wally stepped forward, attired in his Eucharistic vestments, Faith's heart began to thump. She still couldn't believe what she was seeing...this man who had treated her as horribly as he did several years ago was now a "man of the cloth?"

As Wally stepped up to the pulpit to deliver his sermon,

Faith's rapid heartbeat was nearly in the red zone. She was awestruck by what she was seeing and hearing!

Wally began his sermon. "In the name of the Father and of the Son and of the Holy Spirit. May the words of my mouth and the meditation of my heart be acceptable unto thee, my precious Lord. Welcome to St. John's, everyone. I am deeply honored to be invited to worship with you in your beautiful and historic church while your rector, Robert Alves, is attending the Diocesan convention in Wilmington, and hope I will be able to personally meet you at our coffee get-together in the Parish Hall after today's service.

Today is Epiphany Sunday. Epiphany basically means an enlightenment or understanding of things previously unknown to us. In the context of our faith, it alludes to the revealing to the Gentiles of Jesus as the Christ, and we celebrate this important event in our church liturgical calendar.

In our personal lives, we also think of an epiphany as a major revealing of things that greatly matter to us, just as our Lord's recognition as the Christ mattered to the Gentiles. Like I'm sure many of you have experienced in your personal lives, I also had a major epiphany a few years ago in my own life that I will share with you.

I was raised by my mother in this very town of Fayetteville. My father was a criminal who had been in prison, and left us when my siblings and I were small children. I didn't realize it at the time, but most of my behavior after my father left us and my mother had died of alcoholism had been anger-driven because I didn't have a mom or dad like most of the other kids.

I didn't hate God, because I didn't even know Him, but I found myself hating pretty much everyone in my life that I did know. By the time I was eighteen years old, I joined the Army. But my anger and self-pity had become so overwhelming and uncontrolled that I turned to alcohol to medicate my feelings, just as my mother had, and was dishonorably discharged from the service for it.

After that, I entered into a life of nearly total immorality and caused great pain to many good people along the way while I was in that destructive and angry stage of my life. One of those good people may be sitting among you here today.

As I should have been, I was sent off to prison at the age of twenty-one for a multitude of sinful offenses. Then, one night while I was sitting alone in my prison cell, I was thumbing through a Newsweek magazine. In it was a recruiting advertisement from the U.S. Army with a slogan that said, *Be All You Can Be.* Those words suddenly struck every nerve in my mind like a bolt of lightning. I asked myself, is this all I can be...a pathetic piece of humanity who was locked up in a prison cell with no education, no future, and no worthwhile purpose or vision for my life?

The prison chaplain, Reverend Ben Gerrardy, had invited us inmates to a Sunday worship service. At that point in my life, I had never attended any kind of church since I was a small child, but decided I would go only because it was a chance to be out of my cell for awhile, and I heard they served doughnuts and coffee after the service.

As I sat in the prison chapel, the chaplain's message reinforced the feelings that had been planted in my mind from reading the Army recruiting advertisement in the magazine the night before.

He said, "You gentlemen are probably at the very lowest point of your lives...but you don't have to stay there. Whatever wrongs you have done in your past, you can rise above them by seeking God's forgiveness, which

He will give you if you will only sincerely ask Him to, and then direct your God-given minds and bodies to be all you can be...and I hope each of you can be more than a prison inmate with no purpose in your life."

When the Chaplain spoke of how Jesus Christ had also been a condemned prisoner under Pontius Pilate, and was executed on a cross at Calvary for proclaiming to be the Son of God, strange and wonderful thoughts were rumbling inside my mind. I thought to myself, I know I can't be anything like Jesus, but if He had the courage to stand up to death as bravely as He did in being who He was, I can sure try to stand up to and face the obstacles that I had created in my life and try to be whatever I can be.

At the end of the service, the Chaplain asked those of us who wanted to accept and follow Jesus as our Lord and Savior to come forward. I felt as though I was being lifted from my seat by a strange power, probably angels, and led to the altar to make this commitment to our Lord. That was the beginning of a new life in Christ for me.

The Chaplain and I soon became real close friends and he convinced the Seminary to forgive me of my past sinful life and accept me as a student after my early parole, and a true miracle occurred when I graduated and was later ordained.

I pray that any of you who may find yourself lost in your life as I once was will reach out and let Him guide you to where you belong with a new life in Him. We cannot change our past, but we can only ask our Lord for His forgiveness for where we have failed...and then follow Him into a future that can be filled with blessings beyond our greatest imagination. That's what happened to me...it was truly Amazing Grace at its best!

Wally ended his sermon with several concluding

supporting scriptural quotes, and Faith sat in her pew feeling totally awed by what she had heard coming from Wally's lips. When she went forward to receive Holy Communion from him, she was feeling uplifted and better about life than she had in a long while. The painful stigma of those bad memories in Tar Heel seemed to be becoming wiped away from her mind and replaced with a deep respect for Wally...the new and saved Wally.

As he handed her the communion wafer while she knelt, Faith looked up at Wally, smiled at him, and winked; and he recognized her and winked back. Afterwards, at the coffee get-together in the Parish Hall, Faith stood alone on the far side of the hall as the parishioners greeted Wally and expressed their appreciation for his moving sermon.

Faith had an urge to walk up to Wally and hug him, but she somehow lacked the courage. She was still in a state of shock over this incredulous transformation of the man who had once raped and planned to kill her and whom she had once tried to kill from there to where he was now. He looked toward her warmly, smiled, and began walking towards her. She began to tremble inside as he stood before her.

He reached his hand out and gently took hers into both of his. "Hello, Faith. It's so good to see you, and thank you so much for coming. I know it wasn't easy for you, but it means so much to me to see you again, and I have to tell you that you look absolutely great...and I'm so impressed with what I've read about the good work that you're doing."

As they spoke, Faith found herself again engaged in a confusing mental struggle, where she was torn between recalling his phony charm of years ago and how taken in and hurt by him she had been, and in seeing this wonderful and handsome man of God who was even far more charming...and seemingly for real. She gave in to her almost overwhelming feelings of confused anxiety and tightly hugged him.

As they hugged each other, it felt as though a strong surge of electricity was going through her mind and body, and Faith knew she had to leave right away to get her head on straight. With tears beginning to form in her eyes, she waved goodbye to Wally and quickly departed from the church.

# Chapter Fourteen

In the most profoundly confused state of mind she had ever experienced, Faith returned home and immediately put on her running clothes. Running had become her means of escaping from confused or painful feelings and getting her self-control back during the times when she became confronted with too much stress and anxiety. She was emotionally torn with extreme ambivalence in her feelings toward the now *two* most significant men in her life, Tommy and the new Wally.

Prior to setting out on her run, she checked her voice mail and saw that Tommy had called her. Feeling more anxiety over what she would hear, she held her breath as she hit the play button to hear his message, which she assumed wouldn't be a happy one.

"Faith, it's Tommy. First, I want to apologize for leaving you in such a state of anger the way I did at the beach the other day. I do understand your feelings about us and want you to know that I wish you well and hope you will understand and forgive me for doing what I must do.

I was involved in the obesity project with you primarily because of the personal feelings I had for you. Since we're clearly not going to be the couple I had once hoped we would, I have decided it is best for me to make a major change of direction in my life by dropping out of the study of psychology, and studying for a degree in my first love of civil engineering instead. So I'll be transferring to NC State next week. This means that your project is now yours alone.

I now believe you were right in your feelings toward my mother which, from your perspective, I do understand because she does sometimes place too high a value on one's financial and social status. When I returned from the beach, I had a serious talk with her and Dad, and they also feel that we would have made a serious mistake by getting married because of the major difference in our backgrounds. Anyhow, Faith, I do wish you well and a part of me will always love and appreciate you as the wonderful woman that you are. Good luck to you in whatever you choose to do."

Tommy's phone call had brought one major issue facing Faith to a final, although very disappointing, resolution. She realized she still had to sort out her thoughts about Wally and, of more importance to her, determine what she could do in order to continue with her life's work, now that Tommy and his father's important support were no longer there to help.

Thoughts of giving up and gobbling up a box of candy bars were beginning to enter her mind, so off she took off on her run to help wash them and the other issues of negativity, confusion, and anxiety out of her mind.

This run would turn into her longest one ever. She initially ran down Hay Street and through the downtown area of Fayetteville, a distance of about two miles, and then out onto a ten-mile circle around the outskirts of town on Route 87, past the same spot where Wally had picked her up ten years ago, and up Robeson Street, then back to her home.

All the while during her run, Faith was having a mental chat with Jesus, Ruth, John, and Ella Mae Brown to think of what their views of the several issues facing her would be. She returned to her home totally exhausted, but somewhat freed of the strong negative forces that had been acting on her mind prior to starting her run.

\*\*\*

Faith then sat down at her kitchen table with a pen and tablet, and began to scratch out the beginnings of a new plan. She knew she was never going to give up on the pursuit of her self-actualizing life's dream of building a program to help people who are like she had once been in order to be all they could be! She was determined that she was going to climb to the top of that mountain, no matter what it took to get there!

The key questions now facing Faith were to determine how she would do it and what she would need to in order to accomplish it by herself, now that Tommy and his father's financial, influential, and medical support were no longer in the picture.

On one sheet, Faith listed her assets. These included a master's degree in Psychology, pending certification as a licensed professional counselor, the two homes she had inherited from her parents which had a combined value of nearly a half million dollars, and the most important asset of all to her which she wrote in capital letters, was her determination to succeed...*TO BE ALL I CAN BE FOR GOD AND FOR MYSELF!*

On a second sheet, she began to list her liabilities. These included a shortage of cash flow, as she had been struggling to live on the rental income from the Carolina Beach home, which averaged around $1,200. per month and the occasional small cash contributions given by attendees at her seminars that fell way short of her expenses; no one to assist her in the project, and just being plain tired.

She decided her first step should be to enlist at least one other person to join her in her efforts. She pondered this for awhile and came up with three possibilities: a sorority sister from Methodist University whom she had helped to free from her obesity and who was also finishing her master's degree in psychology; a friend from her old church, First Christian Church in Fayetteville, whom she had helped and had volunteered to help if she needed her, and her longtime friend, Cheryl Peters, who probably couldn't spare the time from her busy school job. She had a brief passing thought of considering Wally, but quickly dismissed it as being a highly unlikely and just plain crazy thought.

As she was busily pondering her options, her telephone rang and it was Wally.

"Faith, you have no idea how uplifting and refreshing it was for me to see you at church today, and I really appreciate your coming. You've become a very beautiful lady and the work you're doing really impresses me."

"Why thank you, Wally. It was inspiring for me to hear your wonderful sermon and know of the good things that have happened in your life as well. By the way, in reflecting on your sermon, a small question came up in my mind. When you were talking about your earlier life as a small child, didn't you say that you and your mother lived in a trailer park in Fayetteville?"

"Yes, Faith, we sure did. It was a small single-wide one in the Bonnie Doone area. We lived there for about three years and then moved to a small apartment near the Hope Mills area where my mother worked as a convenience store clerk before she passed away."

"Oh my God, Wally; I think we were neighbors at one time, because my mother and I also lived in a trailer park in Bonnie Doone. Do you recall the name of the trailer park where you and your mother lived? Could it have been the Green Acres Mobile Home Park?"

"Yes, Faith, I'm pretty sure that was the name of where we lived from when I was around five until about the time I turned eight. Now it all comes back to me, and I think I do remember you from then, even though we never spoke to each other because you would've been an infant then, and we moved away shortly afterwards."

Faith said, "Isn't it absolutely amazing how small this world is, Wally?"

"Yes, Faith it really is. We both came from a sad and troubled past that lacked the spiritual content that we both fortunately discovered later in life after going through the hellacious one we had earlier lived. Do you think there's a chance that we might meet for lunch or dinner one day while I'm here?" I know your heart has scars on it which I caused and that may never heal, but I truly do want to see you again as the new person that you've become if that's at all possible."

They agreed they would meet for lunch at the Hilltop House restaurant the next day.

***

When Faith awakened the following morning, she went for her regular run. As she ran, she was experiencing a somewhat irrational mental debate in her mind as to whether or not she should keep her lunch date with Wally.

*What more do we have to talk about? Will he try to rape me again? Does he love me? Do I love him? Is he trying to con me into something? Is he really the changed and spiritually driven guy that he seems to be? Will he play a future role in my life?* Having no clear answers to these critical and troubling questions, she finally decided she should keep her lunch date with him.

When she pulled into the parking lot of the restaurant at the agreed upon time, Faith saw Wally nervously pacing around in front of the Hilltop House. As she walked toward the building, Wally began quickly walking toward her with a wide smile on his face. She felt torn between wanting to run up and hug him and wanting to run away from him as fast as she could...so they hugged, and the hug lasted longer than the typical polite greeting hug.

At lunch, they shared a lot of "polite talk," mostly relating to his work as a clergyman and her work with the obesity project. They did have a couple of light laughs about where they both once lived as small children, but no mention was ever made of the hellish episode she experienced in Tar Heel other than his frequently expressing his regrets for the past behavior of the 'old Wally'.

When they were finished with lunch and preparing to leave the restaurant, Wally asked her, "Do you think there's a chance we might get together again anytime soon, Faith?"

"I think that might be possible, Wally, but don't you have to go back to your church in Elizabethtown today? And do we really have anything else that we need to talk about?" Faith asked.

Wally said, "My church isn't that far away, Faith, and I think we both know that we could benefit from continuing in our conversations. For me, our visit today has been very therapeutic in helping me to better understand why we've both done things in the past that were morally wrong and destructive to both of us and, most of all, how we've both grown from them. I really do admire the wonderful person that you've become and would like to get to know you better."

Faith replied, "I 'kinda feel the same way toward you, Wally, and I'm also glad we had this meeting." They both hugged goodbye, then got into their cars and left.

When Faith arrived back at her home, she realized that she had some major challenges ahead with both getting her vision regarding helping people with obesity to move forward, and working through the feelings she was having about Wally. To quantify it, in her mind she had gone from 99% bad and 1% good to the opposite in her view of Wally. In short, she felt herself being emotionally drawn towards the 'new Wally'.

As she usually did when faced with a dilemma, Faith put on her sneakers and headed out for a meditative run. As she ran, her thoughts were dominated by the two largest issues of the day; putting momentum back into her perceived raison d'être of helping the obese, and having a close, personal relationship with a man with whom she could share mutual respect, love, and trust... the last being a source of anxiety over whether or not Wally might possibly fill the bill. Faith felt very lonely...

Faith heard Ruth's voice in her mind saying to her, "Why don't you take a chance, girl, and see where it goes? What do you have to lose? After all, he's already had you under the worst of circumstances; and perhaps it might be great for you under what looks like some possibly real good ones ahead. Go ahead and give it a try, Honey."

She then heard Ella Mae Brown voice saying, "Child, the boy's done some pretty bad things in his life and so have you; but you've both found the Lord so let Him lead you both. Maybe Wally is the man you need in your life. Remember from our Bible studies together that our Lord told us that we weren't meant to be alone." She turned around and raced home because she felt that she was going to soon find the answer!

Faith called Wally at his church office. He answered,

"St. Alfred's Church, this is Father Wally; how may I help you?" She replied, "By coming to my home in Fayetteville for dinner next Friday night if you're available."

"Wow, Faith; my greatest prayer has just been answered and I'll gladly make myself available!" said Wally. "What time should I come and what may I bring?"

Faith replied, "How about around six-thirty, and just bring yourself."

"I'll surely be there and I'm really looking forward to seeing you again, Faith."

Faith then went on to the next issue on her mind, the obesity project, and found that she was thinking more clearly now that she had made a commitment to resolve her ambivalence about Wally.

She thought to herself, *Maybe I should align myself with an existing organization rather than having to get involved with all the administrative and financial crap needed to start my own program. Heck, maybe Wally might even have some good ideas to consider. Anyhow, I'm going to do this, whatever it takes to get it done.*

\*\*\*

At exactly six-thirty on Friday evening, her doorbell rang. It was Wally, who was dressed in a neat light grey suit and wore a clerical collar. He smiled, they briefly hugged, and he handed her a small, attractive bouquet of flowers for which Faith thanked him.

Faith was attired in an attractive and very conservative flowered print dress, and looked gorgeous. She had prepared a dinner of baked flounder with a large, loaded salad, and had iced tea for their beverage, which she served on her home's outdoor rear deck.

The two of them sat outside and had a nice chat while they sipped their iced tea. Recalling his past drinking of beer, Faith had bought a six-pack of beer to offer Wally. She asked if he'd prefer beer or something else to drink, to which he replied, "Tea is now my favorite beverage, Faith; thanks for remembering, but I don't use the nasty alcohol stuff any longer. The only alcoholic beverage for me now is the communion wine, and that's only a few sips on Sunday."

After they finished with dinner, the sun had set and they continued to share their interesting stories over a healthy dessert of crushed pineapple, strawberries, and grapes about things that had happened to each of them after the Tar Hell episode of several years past. Finally, Faith asked him in a serious tone, "I need to know something, Wally, and I don't want to offend you, but please tell me your real reason for wanting to spend these times with me?"

"What do you mean by my real reason, Faith? Do I need to have a special reason, other than what we've shared, to pursue a friendship with you, which I'm finding to be very enjoyable and uplifting? You are a beautiful, highly moral, and very intelligent woman whom I enjoy knowing and with whom I would like to have a continuing friendship. Isn't that reason enough?

I'll admit that my initial reason was to know that you had survived from the horrible way I treated you many years ago, and for which I shall never be able to forgive myself, but it has quickly escalated into something much more important than that for me."

Both Faith and Wally were beginning to feel somewhat awkward and uneasy with the direction their conversation had been taking when Wally changed the subject by asking, "Where do you stand with your fabulous idea of helping people who suffer with obesity, Faith?"

She replied, "I'm really not sure at this point, Wally. I had gotten a little momentum building for it with the medical community until a few days ago when my former partner in the project decided that it wasn't for him and opted out, taking my financial support and medical contacts away, so I'm now in the process of putting a new plan together. One way or another, I still feel so strong about it that I'm sure I'll find a way to make it happen."

"Have you ever considered doing it as a ministry within the church?" Wally asked.

Faith replied, "No, I hadn't thought of that, Wally, but I would think that the need is definitely there, like it is everywhere in our society. Do you think the church might have an interest in participating in it?"

"I don't know, Faith, but I'll be glad to look into the possibility of it for you. Your work excites me, too, and I personally think it could be a great outreach ministry for the church to pursue."

Wally began checking his watch several times and finally said, "I have really enjoyed our visit and the delicious dinner, Faith, but I'd better be moving on since I have to get up early for an 8:30 a.m. service tomorrow. They both sensed that they had accomplished a great deal during this visit, and that it should end on a positive note...with, hopefully, more good ones to follow.

# Chapter Fifteen

Both Faith's and Wally's dreams that night were of each other. They contained a mixture of happy thoughts involving future possibilities for their relationship, along with an occasional unsettling flashback to the less pleasant times in their lives. Fortunately, the former types of thoughts dominated both of their dreams and they slept well with encouraging thoughts.

At noon on the following day, Faith's doorbell rang. It was a delivery man from Dale's Florist Shop with a dozen beautiful red roses. The card inside read, "Thank you for a truly wonderful evening and a delicious dinner, Faith. God was certainly with us and I believe He will always stay. Love, Wally."

The word, *love,* was huge to Faith because, although it was anxiety producing, love is exactly what she was feeling the beginnings of towards the man whom she had once hated and wanted to kill. It was definitely time for another long run and a serious chat with the loving and wiser spirits of Jesus, Ruth, and Ella Mae!

As she ran, she prayed. "Dear Jesus, You have always been there for me when I needed a compass to show me the way to go in my life, and I really need to know which way I should go where Wally is concerned.

If Wally really is what he appears to be, he is definitely

the most wonderful man I've ever met. Please clear my mind of the fear I have that he could be fooling me again and, if he really is the right man for me, I ask your blessing upon both of us."

To Ruth and Ella Mae, she said, "You two have always had my back and protected me with your wisdom, love, and better judgment, and I need your support more now than I ever have before."

Ella Mae's voice first came into her mind. "You've done hit your sweet self a home run with your man, child, so go for it because I believe he's the one for you; the one you need to be really happy and get things done the way you want them done." She heard Ruth's voice render an "Amen to that, gal!"

***

Faith had to prepare for a drive to the small town of Monroe, North Carolina and give her presentation at an event sponsored by the local Rotary Club that had been scheduled by Tommy and his father a month before.

She packed her suitcase, slide projector, and equipment in her car early the next morning and arrived in Monroe just before noon. The Club President, retired financial guru, Les Wandler, and his lovely tennis professional wife, Susan, met them at the Monroe Holiday Inn where the event was to be held.

Mr. Wandler asked Faith where her colleague, Dr. Jordan's son, Tommy, was and told her that he and Dr. Jordan were old personal friends and fellow Rotarians. Faith replied, "I'm sorry, sir, but your club will just have me today as Tommy won't be able to make it."

She could tell from the look on his face that Mr. Wandler wasn't very happy about the situation since he had promoted the event to the club as a favor to his friend, Dr. Jordan, and was obviously unaware that the Jordan's were no longer involved with the project.

But Faith, being the trouper that she was, handled the awkward situation quite well and quickly won over the Club and its President. In fact, after her powerful one-hour presentation was over and she received a standing ovation, Mr. Wandler presented Faith with a nice and unexpected contribution from the club of a thousand dollars and the Wandler's personal donation of another thousand dollars! This success helped to pump up Faith's confidence and pocketbook, and reinforced her commitment to stay the course with the project, even without Tommy's or his father's help.

***

When Faith returned to Fayetteville early that evening, she had two voice mail messages; one from Tommy and another from Wally.

Tommy said, "I'm sorry that I forgot to let the Monroe Rotary Club know about my no longer being on your team, Faith. Mr. Wandler, who's an old friend of my dad, called and raised hell about my not being there before the meeting started, but then called again after your presentation and said you did a terrific job.

So, see, you really didn't need me after all. We had two more presentations scheduled, one in Charlotte and another in High Point, but I took the liberty of calling and cancelling both of them. Good luck, Faith."

Tommy's call really pissed Faith off, but she realized there was nothing she could do about it. This low blow from Tommy lit a fire under her to revamp her plan and get whatever she decided to do in motion real quick.

Wally had also called that afternoon and left her a message that he had discussed her program with the

Bishop of Eastern North Carolina's Director of Outreach Programs and he had expressed a strong interest in it.

"Can you and I get together day after tomorrow and meet with him, Faith? He'll be here in Elizabethtown and would like to have lunch with us." *Us?*, thought Faith. *Could that mean that Wally has an interest in becoming involved with me in the project?* This thought caused a small resurgence of her uneasy ambivalence, but she called Wally and accepted his invitation.

\*\*\*

Two days later, Faith drove to Elizabethtown to meet with Wally and the Diocese's Outreach Director, Reverend Rick Lindsey. They met in Wally's church office where a nice light lunch had been prepared for them. Faith provided Reverend Lindsey with a package describing her program and he seemed impressed with it. He asked, "Miss Thomas, are you interested in running all the presentations you make by yourself, or would you also consider training others to present it?"

"That's a good question, Reverend Lindsey, and to tell you the truth I hadn't even considered conducting a train-the-trainer program, but it does make good sense and I'll give it some thought. On the surface, though, I don't think it would be a problem for me to do it that way," said Faith.

Rev. Lindsey seemed satisfied with Faith's response and was obviously impressed with her and her ideas. He assured her that he would get back to her within a few days with a decision. He said he leaned toward conducting a train-the-trainer program instead of having Faith conduct them all "because it would give us wider coverage and more flexibility, and will probably attract the attention and interest of other dioceses around the country."

After Reverend Lindsey left them, Wally complimented Faith on the professionalism of her presentation and asked if she would like his help in putting the suggested program together. He added, "Have you ever considered writing a book about this, Faith?"

Faith replied, "I would like to do that if and when I can ever find the time to do it, Wally."

Wally added, "I really believe you would have a best-seller on your hands if you did it because, as you pointed out in your presentation, this is a major problem throughout our society, and this way you could reach more people all over the world instead of just a few in our small North Carolina stomping ground."

Faith replied, "I'll have to give some more thought to that idea, Wally, because this would be a totally new approach and one that will require some major revamping of what I've been doing, and I'll let you know. I've got to head back for home now, but I'll talk with you later. Thanks so much for your help." She gave him a hug goodbye and left.

On her drive back, she pondered the idea that had been suggested about writing a book and the more she thought of the idea, the more it appealed to her. By the time she reached home, she had all but decided to do exactly that and couldn't wait to get to her computer and start writing!

Faith was glad to see that no one had left a message while she was away, as most of her recent ones had been nothing but bad news. She took out her old notebook of things she considered to be used if she should ever choose to write a book, and sat down at her computer to begin writing. By midnight, she was still writing and had already written nearly fifty pages and was on a roll! She finally fell asleep at her desk at two in the morning.

The next morning, Faith went for her daily run and ran faster than normal because she couldn't wait to return to her writing project. Although she was an excellent typist, her enthusiastic thinking was running faster than her fingers could type. As the sun began to set, she had already pounded out a hundred pages.

Wally called at a little after six that evening and asked how the project was going.

Faith said, "Unbelievable, Wally! I already have a hundred pages done and I'm just getting started. I'm guessing that this is going to be at least three to four hundred pages before I can get it done. Do you have any more wonderful suggestions for me, your greatness?"

"Yeah, Lady Faith, I don't know what form you have it in, but I think it would be fantastic if you could make it an *experiential* one rather than a textbook kind of thing. I think people would relate more to it that way and you'd still be getting your points across to the readers."

"That's pretty much the way I'm doing it, Wally...'kinda like a novel with lots of meaty stuff for the reader to relate to. I envision it being sort of like Ayn Rand's classic, *Atlas Shrugged,* was...a story that makes heavy points for the reader's consumption."

Wally asked, "Do you have someone in mind to help you edit it?"

"No, Wally, I hadn't thought about that. Why would I need an editor?"

Wally replied, "Because you should have an objective-minded person with strong literary skills to review and critique it before you run it up the flagpole for the literary agents to see. I understand that getting your book published in today's competitive market is a huge challenge.

There's another thing that I haven't shared with you yet, Faith, but I've also been working on a book that deals with the power of spirituality and I've discovered just how steep and difficult the publishing mountain is to climb. I've been working on this one for over a year and have just about decided to self-publish it if I don't get a favorable response from an agent soon. The next time we're together, I'll show you my manuscript."

"When will the next time be, Wally?" Faith asked.

Wally replied, "How about day after tomorrow for lunch? I've got to be in Fayetteville to pick up some things for the church at Office Depot. How about meeting me for lunch at the old Huske Hardware restaurant on Hay Street around noon?"

"I'll be there waiting for you, sir," Faith cheerfully replied.

When he arrived at noon on the following day, Faith was pleased that she was no longer experiencing her flashback anxiety over seeing Wally and was, in fact, eagerly looking forward to being with him! He was waiting for her in front of the restaurant.

After they were seated at their restaurant table, Wally said grace then asked, "Well, my great authoress, how's America's soon to be Number One best seller coming?"

Faith replied, "It's coming along okay, Wally, but it's not nearly as easy a task as I had initially envisioned. I write and write, but when I go back over what I've written, I usually wind up rewriting most of what I've previously written, and I do it over and over.

As dumb as it may sound, I actually thought I could knock out a book in a matter of a few days. Now it looks like it's going to take me several months to get it done right! Tell me about your experience, Wally."

"Well, Faith, after I had finished - or *thought* I had finished the first six chapters - I floated it out to several agents to see if I could garner some interest. Those are the people that a writer pretty much has to go through in order to get anything before the major publishers. So I waited, waited, and waited for their reply, but nothing ever happened...not even a no-thank-you letter or anything. Then a good friend of mine educated me on the realities of publishing a book and I realized just how difficult it is."

"What about self-publishing, Wally? Have you looked into that?"

"That's an option, Faith, but it can be expensive and you pretty much have to do your own promoting of it by doing book signings and lots of other stuff that sucks up a lot of your time...much more time than my work would allow me to give to it."

Wally then opened his brief case and withdrew a manuscript that looked to be around 300+ pages. "I brought you a copy of my work in progress if you'd like to check it out, Faith. I have to warn you that there's some pretty bad stuff in it about the old me that you may recognize and find upsetting, but I didn't name names and kept it in fictional form."

Faith thanked him and they departed with Faith feeling an even deeper attraction for Wally and him for her.

# Chapter Sixteen

A couple of days had passed since they had lunch and Faith's mind was constantly divided between having good thoughts of Wally and focusing on her work. At Wally's recommendation, Faith had contracted with a former college English professor in Florida by the name of Ruthi Seward to edit her writing.

Faith had become deeply immersed in her work and hadn't found the time to look at the manuscript which Wally had given her. She had mixed feelings about reading it as well, because she was fearful that he might have included some details about his awful experience with her that she would recognize and they might serve to reopen the healing wounds in her mind.

Early one morning before starting on her work, she finally gave in to her curiosity and picked up Wally's manuscript. In his foreword, he expressed his deep remorse and apologies to those whom he had hurt in his past life, "especially a sad and hurting young girl who trusted me and whom I badly hurt, a sin for which I shall forever be ashamed."

She then went on and read the complete manuscript, and was glad their past unfortunate experience wasn't described in all its gory detail. The main focus was in what he described as a "rebirth in God," which was similar in its theme to his recent sermon at St. John's, and was very touching.

Faith was so moved by Wally's manuscript that she picked up the phone and called him. The church secretary answered the phone and Faith asked to speak with Reverend (she still couldn't believe it as she said the word, *Reverend*) Cochran. The secretary said he was not available, but she would take her name and number and give it to him when he was finished with another task. When she heard Faith's name, she said, "Wait a minute, Miss Thomas. Reverend Cochran told me that I was to interrupt him and put your call through to him when you call, regardless of what he was doing."

After a few seconds, Wally answered. "Hi there, Faith, how's the project going?"

Hearing Wally's cheerful voice was uplifting and made Faith feel good inside, especially that he had regarded phone calls from her as being of such a high priority! She said, "I just wanted you to know that I finished reading your manuscript, Wally, and I think it's an absolutely fantastic piece of work!"

"Well thank you, dear lady. Your opinion means even more to me than a potential publisher's. How are you coming with yours?" Wally asked.

"I sure have learned what the term, *writer's block*, means, Wally, but I'm struggling along and just passed the two hundred page mark. I got in touch with your Florida friend, Ruthi Seward, and she has been a really great help in cleaning up my literary screw ups and helping me to restructure a lot of it so it would make better sense to a reader. Thanks a million for recommending her to me."

"You're mighty welcome, lovely lady. When might I have the pleasure of your company again, Faith? I really do miss you."

Faith said, "You miss me? Good gosh, Wally, we had lunch together just two days ago."

"I know, Faith, but I still miss you and enjoy our get-togethers so much that I'm becoming addicted to being with you. I just can't help it."

As much as she was enjoying the "new Wally," Faith would still sometimes subconsciously find herself putting her developing good feelings towards him on guard when he said such nice things to her.

One evening as she lay in her bed, Faith was finding herself feeling the same way towards Wally as he had expressed feeling towards her...missing him terribly. So, now feeling much more comfortable about calling him than she had previously felt, she dialed his home number and he answered on the first ring as he always did.

"Okay, Wally, you win...because I'm missing you too. It's supposed to be a pretty weekend at Carolina Beach, and I'm thinking about driving down to my parents' place for a couple of days before it's rented again and go for a relaxing run on the beach. Would you care to join me?"

Wally replied, "Would I? Why I'd rather do that than drive to Raleigh to collect on a million dollar lottery ticket! When do you want to go and what can I bring? Shall I pick you up at your home?"

Faith said, "That won't be necessary, Wally, since I have to go through Elizabethtown on the way there, and you don't need to bring a thing. Why don't we meet at your church and go in my car from there?"

"Sounds like a plan to me, Faith...and a great one! What time should I expect you, my dear chauffeur?"

Faith said, "How about around Noon on Friday afternoon? I know you have to be back for your service on Sunday morning, so that'll give us a couple of days to do a little running on the beach and doing some literary brainstorming together."

*Edward Vaughn*

"I'm looking forward to it, Faith, and I'll see you at Noon on Friday at the church."

\*\*\*

When Friday morning came, Faith excitedly rose from her bed and took off on her daily run, where she had happy thoughts about spending some extended time with Wally, then returned and began packing for the trip to Carolina Beach.

She arrived at St. Alfred's Church where she found Wally waiting for her in front with a small bag and a laptop computer in a case. He was wearing black and white plaid shorts, a black tee shirt, and dark sunglasses... and looked so cool and handsome to Faith!

They got into Faith's car and stopped for lunch in the small town of Riegelwood en route; then headed south towards Wilmington, and finally arrived at Carolina Beach. They went into the beach "palace," and put their bags into separate bedrooms.

When Faith went into her bedroom, she screamed, "Help, Wally, come here quick...there's a strange man sleeping in my bed!"

When Wally rushed in, the obviously drunken intruder jumped up, pulled a knife out of his pocket, and tried to grab Faith, threatening to kill her. Wally quickly kicked the knife out of the intruder's hand and knocked him out cold with one punch. He then called the Carolina Beach police, who came and took the intruder off to jail.

Faith was trembling with fear from the experience and Wally held her close until she settled down. She said with deep admiration, "Thank you so much, my hero, for saving my life! I could've been killed if you hadn't been here to save me."

Wally said, "I'm just glad I was with you and you didn't come here alone. Most of all, I'm glad you're okay."

It was a beautiful day with temperatures in the mid-seventies and, after she had settled down from the earlier harrowing experience, Faith asked Wally if he would like to join her for a run on the beach, which he accepted.

Faith said, "I have to warn you that I've been running every day for years, usually twice, Wally; so don't be afraid to stop if you get tired before I do."

Wally replied laughingly, "Let's get it on, Miss Marathon. Another thing I don't think I've told you is that I also go for a run every day. I started doing it back while I was in prison eight years ago and haven't missed a day since, so don't *you* be afraid to stop if *you* tire out before *I* do!"

"Okay, my great hero, you're on. Let's go!" said Faith with a giggle.

They had both been running together from one end of the beach to the other, a distance of nearly five miles, when Wally finally said, "Okay, Faith, that's about enough running for me right now, so I've got to stop and let you win the race, madam!"

Faith said, "Wow, Wally; thank goodness you stopped, because I was about to throw in the towel myself. Did you quit running just to make me feel good or were you really pooped out? Come on now and be honest with me."

Wally smiled and said, "I'm not saying...my lips are sealed! Actually, I was worn out, so you really did win the race, Faith. Would you mind if this old man holds your hand while we walk back to the house?"

Faith told him she would be honored to hold the powerful hand that knocked the intruder out and they laughed as they walked together back to the house, hand in hand.

Once inside, Wally took out his laptop computer and

showed Faith some interesting web sites for her to use in contacting writers' agents, which she copied down. He asked how her writing project was going, and Faith told him it was going very well now that Ruthi Seward, the woman he had recommended to her as an editor, was helping her.

They sat outside on the porch sipping cold iced tea while listening to some soothing music that Wally played on his computer. Wally leaned toward her and said, "Faith, I know you're probably tired of hearing me express my apologies to you for the way I treated you ten years ago, but I can't help it. You'll never know how deeply I regret the way I behaved then."

Faith sat up and assertively said, "Wally, if you apologize to me one more time, I'm going to scream! That part of our lives is over with and we're where we are now. Let's go forward in our thinking and leave the past behind us."

"And where is that, Faith? Where are we now from your point of view?" asked Wally.

"I think you know where we are, Wally, don't you?"

"No, Faith, please tell me where you think we are."

Faith took a deep breath and said, "Well, Wally, I have to be honest and tell you I'm falling in love with you, and that's the last thing that I ever expected would happen to me."

"Thank God," Wally exclaimed. "Hearing those words from you make me the happiest I've ever been in this life, because I'm in love with you too."

"Then if you love me, how about kissing me, Wally?"

Wally walked over to Faith's chair, held her, and gave her the softest and sweetest kiss on her lips; then slowly withdrew and looked into her eyes with a warm smile on his face." He went no further in expressing his affection to Faith then, and asked if he could take her out for a seafood dinner.

"Yes, sir, that would be a good thing for us to do and I know the perfect place that serves the best seafood on the island," said Faith.

Over a delicious lobster tail dinner, they chatted about her book, which Faith said she expected to bring to closure within the coming month or so.

Wally asked, "What have you chosen as a title of your soon to be best seller, Faith?"

"Run for Your Life," Faith replied, "because running has been my life-changing thing for me, my adopted mother's, and to my happy surprise, even yours. I feel that we all need a strong habit like that to motivate us to be and do whatever it is we desire out of our lives, and my readers will be primarily women, and even a few men as well, who have been handicapped by obesity like I once was."

"I love it," said Wally. "I can't think of a more appropriate title for what you're writing about. In what format are you writing it, Faith; like is it an autobiography, novel, or textbook?"

"All of the above," replied Faith. "That's what my editor suggested."

They walked back to the house and Faith asked Wally if he would like to say a prayer with her before they went to their bedrooms.

They held hands and Wally began. "Dear heavenly Father, we thank you for the wonderful blessing you have bestowed upon us by bringing us together in a growing love for each other, and for giving us the joy of sharing our mutual love for You and Your Son, Jesus. Please help us to live the good life, which You have generously given us as You would have us do, and please help us to be all we can be. In Your Holy name we pray." They both said, "Amen."

Faith looked Wally in the eye and said, "I hope you can understand why we must sleep in separate bedrooms, Wally, and aren't disappointed or angry."

Wally replied, "No, dear Faith, I'm not at all annoyed, and I wouldn't have it any other way. If and when you and I should ever sleep together again, I hope it will be as man and wife."

Faith wasn't ready to discuss this new expression of Wally's feelings, and then gave him a warm kiss and wished him good night. They both then went to their individual rooms for the night and slept well.

Early the next morning, Faith knocked on Wally's door and found him already up and dressed for their planned morning run.

It was one of those breathtakingly fabulous days at Carolina Beach, where the bright sun was reflecting on the water like billions of shining diamonds, the waves were exceptionally tall and roaring, and the beautiful beach was immaculate when Faith and Wally began their run. They ran to the far end of the island and chose to walk back, hand in hand, along the water's edge.

As they walked along in a few inches of water, Faith asked Wally, "Did you really mean what you said to me last night, Wally, about your hoping we would someday be man and wife?"

"I sure did, and you can treat that as an official proposal of marriage, Faith."

They suddenly stopped and embraced, and began to exchange even deeper kisses than they had the night before, when a large wave suddenly struck and knocked them both down into the water.

They stood up laughing, and spitting out salt water

when Faith smilingly said, "Then I accept your proposal; so where's my engagement ring, sir?"

"It's coming, my dear lady...it's coming as soon as I can scrape up enough dough to buy you a really nice one. On my measly salary, I couldn't afford a ring around my bath tub right now!" They both hugged and laughed, and Faith assured him that she would gladly wait for the ring, or even do without it if buying one would be a financial burden for him.

They returned to the house, happily skipping along on the beach hand in hand like two little children without a care in the world. Wally checked his cell phone and saw that he had a message. He checked it and found it was the church secretary calling to let him know that one of the key parishioners of the church had been in an automobile accident and was in critical condition at the Elizabethtown Hospital. The church's rector was fully committed to another project and wanted Wally to go to the hospital and help console the man's family.

Wally said, "I'm so sorry, Honey, but it's an emergency and I have to get back to Elizabethtown as quickly as possible to help one of my parishioners and his family. Please forgive me."

"Forgive you for doing what's right, Wally? No forgiveness is necessary. I'm so proud of you for what you do, and we can hit the road right now."

# Chapter Seventeen

When Faith returned to her home in Fayetteville and sorted through her mail, she was pleased to have received a letter expressing interest in the submission of her first three chapters from a major publishing company's literary agent, and she was thrilled!

She called Wally on his cell phone and shared the good news. He told her he would be in Fayetteville most of the day to provide grief counseling for the family of his church member who had since died at the hospital, and asked if she would join him for dinner that evening when he was finished. She enthusiastically accepted his invitation.

That evening, they enjoyed a fabulous dinner at the Hilltop House Restaurant. Afterwards, Wally knelt down before Faith, reached into his pocket and withdrew a beautiful two karat diamond engagement ring he had purchased for her earlier that day from Rhudy's Jewelers.

He asked her, "Will you marry me, Faith, and make me the happiest man alive?"

Faith said, "You know full well I will, Wally. I love you more than you'll ever know and you've made me the happiest woman alive by coming back into my life."

As he slipped the engagement ring on her finger, he said, "And I adore you as well, my precious Faith."

Faith smiled and said, "You sure didn't waste any time getting the ring for me, did you? It's so beautiful and I really appreciate it, but I thought you were broke."

With a chuckle, Wally replied, "I am, but didn't want to risk your changing your mind from last night, and the payments on it will probably last at least through our fifth anniversary!"

After he drove Faith to her home and was preparing to leave for Elizabethtown, she said to him, "Since it's so late, would you like to stay over at my place tonight, even though I only have one bedroom?"

Wally replied, "Sure, Sweetheart, that's probably a good idea because I am sort of whipped out, and I don't mind sleeping on your couch."

Faith smiled and said to him in a come-hither manner, "That's not exactly what I have in mind, Wally. I have a queen-sized bed that'll comfortably allow us to snuggle together and keep each other warm through the night."

To her surprise, Wally declined her seductive invitation. "Nothing would be more joyful to me than for you and I to go to bed together, my precious Faith; but I think we both want that to be something for us to look forward to on our wedding night."

Faith said, "But we've already done that, Wally, and you already have my virginity."

Wally lovingly replied, "Yes, my dearest, the old, immature and unsaved Wally and a poor and young Faith did a lot of things before that they'll never do again and, as much as I want to make love with you, I prefer to honor you by waiting and sharing our *new* virginity as the moral-minded followers of God's Word that we've both become."

Although it seemed strange to hear Wally talking this

way, it deeply impressed her and made her want him even more; but they exchanged a warm and loving kiss and went off to their separate sleeping places.

Early the next morning before Faith had awakened; Wally left a note for her and headed back to Elizabethtown. It read: *Thank you so very much for the two most wonderful days of my life, Faith, and I gratefully and excitedly look forward to becoming your husband and sharing a good life with you forever. All my adoring love <u>always</u> to you, my beautiful wife to be. Your Wally*

***

Faith put on her running gear and headed out for her usual morning run. As she ran, she felt so inspired and uplifted in thinking about this forthcoming major event in her life and had happy visions of her new life with Wally. In her mind, she envisioned her and Wally at the altar; with him in a tuxedo and she in a beautiful, white wedding dress, but then some negative thoughts began to enter her mind.

The first negative thought was that *a white dress is supposed to symbolize virginity and it would be hypocritical of me to present myself at the altar as a virgin when I'm not, wouldn't it?* She thought of what Ruth and Ella Mae would say in reply...*Honey, you really are a virgin in your new life and so is Wally, so enjoy the reward that the self-discipline in your new lives has earned for both of you.*

A second negative thought then entered her mind. *It's only been a little over two months since Wally and I started seeing each other and that's mighty quick. Maybe we should wait awhile before we make any announcements. What will Tommy and his family think about my getting married to someone so soon after we ended our relationship?"* She heard Ruth's voice saying,

"Girl, are you crazy? You'd better grab him while you can and don't worry yourself about what anyone else thinks." This reasoning satisfied her, so she smiled and continued on with one of her happiest runs ever.

***

Wally called early the next morning. "Good morning, Beautiful! I have an important question to ask of you. "When and where would you like to have our wedding?"

Faith was happy to hear Wally's reaffirmation of his proposal and said, "I don't know, Honey, tell me when and where you would like for it to be. Anywhere and anytime you choose will work for me."

"Okay then, how about let's get married *tonight*, and anywhere you'd like?" Wally laughingly asked.

"Why do we have to wait so long?" Faith laughingly responded.

Wally said, "I've been thinking about a significant date for us to be married, and I came up with September the ninth."

"Why did you choose that particular day?" Faith asked.

"Because I figured that's the date you and I first met on the highway nearly ten years ago. Does choosing that day bother you?" Wally asked.

Faith said, "Like I told you, Wally, any day you want is okay with me, and the sooner the better. I can't wait!"

"Okay, then that's it. I'll get a wedding announcement put together by our church printer and fax the draft over for your approval sometime next week, Madam."

As soon as she hung up the phone, Faith's fax machine rang and out popped the draft announcement, and it pleased Faith not only because of his enthusiasm for their marriage, but also for his great sense of humor.

> *Miss Faith Anne Thomas*
> *and*
> *Reverend Wallace Morgan Cochran*
> *Happily announce they will exchange the vows of*
> *Holy Matrimony*
> *at Noon on*
> *Saturday, September 9th, 2000*
> *St. Alfred's Episcopal Church*
> *Elizabethtown, North Carolina*
> *A reception will follow in the Parish Hall*
> *Everyone is welcome to join us on this*
> *wonderful and blessed occasion!*

When Faith saw the draft wedding announcement, she was elated and immediately called Wally. "It's absolutely fabulous, Honey, but I can't understand why it took you so long! I'm teasing, but you know the date you've chosen is only a month from now, so I've got to get my butt in motion and throw some wedding rags together, especially since you've chosen high noon for the ceremony because that's the most formal time of all, you know. Who will marry us, a Justice of the Peace?" she jokingly asked.

"Hey, my dearest bride to be, you deserve the very best and I will see if we can get the Bishop of Eastern North Carolina to do the honors," Wally said.

After she hung up the telephone, Faith's mind was spinning. *I've got to get a wedding dress, figure who will walk me down the aisle and give me away to Wally, plan the reception, and who knows what else...and I only have less than a month to get it all done....arghhhh! I think it's time for me to take a chill-out run...*

When she returned from her chill-out run, the postman had delivered the mail and there was an envelope from one of the major publishing companies. Breathlessly and with trembling hands, she tore open the envelope.

It contained a three page contract for the publishing of her book with the promise of an advance royalty check of ten thousand dollars! As she danced around in circles with the letter in her hand, she happily screamed at the top of her lungs, "Thank You, dear God...thank You!"

She called Wally and Cheryl to share the good news with them and they were also elated, and both told her they would come right over to celebrate this wonderful event. After they enjoyed a great evening of happy celebration and chatting together and Cheryl had left, Wally said he was too whipped to risk driving back home right then, so he stretched out on Faith's sofa for a little shuteye. Faith then laid down beside him with her head resting on his strong shoulder and they fell fast asleep together.

*** 

A couple of weeks later, St. Alfred's Episcopal Church in Elizabethton was filled to capacity by their many friends who had come from all over the state and beyond to attend Faith and Wally's wedding.

Faith chose to be walked down the aisle by the Reverend Maurice Johnson, the minister from the Beulah A.M.E. church in Wilmington whose inspirational sermon of ten years prior began her transformation, and she proudly wore a beautiful white lace wedding gown. Cheryl Peters and Elizabeth Sasser served as her matrons of honor, and Wally's old prison chaplain, Reverend Ben Gerrardy, served as his best man.

Clarice Shaw, the woman whom Faith had befriended

and turned her life around several years ago while she was in jail with her, and who had later become a highly successful professional singer after winning *The American Idol*, traveled from Los Angeles, California for the occasion and sang a solo of Amazing Grace.

After the wedding and the joyful but conservative and non-alcoholic reception in the church hall were over, Faith and Wally headed for their wonderful week-long honeymoon at Tybee Island, Georgia where they more than made up for lost time with their richly satisfying lovemaking in a luxurious beachfront hotel suite, on the beach, in the ocean, and anywhere else they could find!

Exactly nine months to the day later, their first child, a daughter whom they named Ruth, was born and she was a princess of the highest order. One year later, their second child, a son whom they named Wallace, Jr., would be born and was a perfect little prince! Their third beautiful child, another daughter, was named Cheryl, their fourth, another beautiful daughter, was named Ella Mae, and their fifth, a son whom they named John. All five children would become extraordinary achievers... and avid runners!

Wally was later called to serve as the rector of the same large church in Wilmington that John Dickson had served in as the rector for over forty years. They lived in the beautiful home she had inherited from the Dickson's.

Wally hired an investigator who located his two lost siblings, a brother and sister who were living in Asheville, and with whom he and Faith enjoyed a great, lifelong relationship.

Faith published six best-seller books, which focused on acquiring and maintaining a healthy mind and body, and gave frequent lectures and book signings in various parts of the country. Wally and their children always went on the trips with her, using the trips as enjoyable mini-vacations.

Wally and Faith had finally reached the top of their tall mountain together and had truly become *all they could be.*

# Chapter Eighteen

# Excerpts from Faith's first Book, *Run for Your Life:*

- You will know that forgiveness has begun inside your soul when you recall those who once hurt you and begin to feel the power and desire to wish them well.

- To enjoy good health, to bring true happiness to one's family, and to bring peace to all in one's life, one must first discipline and control one's own mind and body. If a person can develop control of his/her mind and body, he/she can find the path to enlightenment, and much wisdom and virtue will naturally come to him/her.

- Criticism may not always be welcome, but it is often necessary and beneficial. It serves the same function for the human mind as pain does for the human body by calling attention to an unhealthy state of things.

- We are made wise not by recalling and living in

the past, but by learning from our mistakes and acting responsibly by focusing on our future. To avoid future wrecks, we should focus on the road ahead and not the one behind us.

- Perseverance is not one long race but instead is many short races one after the other.

- Run away from negative thoughts, and replace them only with positive ones.

- Depression is internalized anger felt toward one's self.

- Almost anything we say or do while we are angry usually proves to be the worst thing. As the great philosopher, Socrates, said, "Those whom the gods seek to destroy, they first made angry."

- Without love there can be no forgiveness; and without forgiveness there can be no love.

- The three most important core elements of one's psyche are intelligence, positive emotions, and a strong and deeply felt spiritual connection.

- A good head and a good heart are a winning combination.

- Each day is like a new canvas upon which to paint. Make certain that your daily painting is a masterpiece filled with positive thoughts.

- There are three critical elements for success: Identifying one's goals, making a deeply inspired and spiritually driven commitment to their achievement, and maintaining a dogged and unending drive toward their accomplishment. In other *words, discovering, committing, and doing!*

• Being overweight is a sin against oneself and the Creator of our bodies, and reflects nothing but a plain old uncaring laziness and self-anger.

• Our bodies and minds are a team which, when properly synchronized, will lead us to be all we can be.

• The worst thing a person can do is to not have any aspirations for their future life; then later spend years in silent pain wondering if something great might have materialized and never even knowing what it might have been.

• Fat people aren't jolly; they're mad and sad.

• Those who deny that God is real are pathetic fools with no basis for hope.

• Of all the many mental disorders, there is none worse or more harmful than anger.

• Resentment and anger do little harm the person towards whom you have such feelings but they do bring much harm to the person who embraces them.